# about the house

## AN INTRODUCTION TO HOME ECONOMICS

**Helen McGrath**

D1354445

Oxford University Press

**Oxford University Press, Walton Street, Oxford OX2 6DP**

Oxford London Glasgow
New York Toronto Melbourne Auckland
Kuala Lumpur Singapore Hong Kong Tokyo
Delhi Bombay Calcutta Madras Karachi
Nairobi Dar es Salaam Cape Town

and associated companies in
Beirut Berlin Ibadan Mexico City Nicosia

*Oxford* is a trade mark of Oxford University Press

First published 1980
Reprinted with corrections 1980, 1981, 1982, 1983, 1984

Printed and bound in Great Britain by
William Clowes Limited,
Beccles and London

# Preface

**About the house** is designed to cover in one book all the material required by the various C.S.E. home economics syllabuses.

The book contains ten chapters, each of which is broken down into a number of self-contained double-page units. Each of these covers a particular topic and ends with questions designed to reinforce understanding of the main teaching points. Notes made from answers to these questions can serve as a basis for future revision.

The sections at the end of each chapter provide an opportunity for further work. The questions here are not meant to be worked through consecutively, but to suggest ideas from which the teacher may select work for discussion, homework or individual project work. Practice in answering examination questions is included.

The book should be of real value to the teacher in the classroom. The double-page units ensure flexibility: as each unit is self-contained, the teacher can cover or omit different topics according to the needs and abilities of a particular group. The book is written in clear, simple language, and is sufficiently comprehensive and self-explanatory to be used when necessary by pupils working on their own. This is particularly useful in a subject like home economics, where practical work is often carried out at the same time and in the same room as theory. The teacher can set her pupils written work which they can carry out unaided while she concentrates on practical work.

**About the house** has been written with the needs of C.S.E. candidates particularly in mind, but it can also be used to provide a concise summary of basic information for O-level examinations.

## Acknowledgements

Illustrations are by Patricia Capon, Marion Mills and Lynne Willey.
The back cover illustration is by Stephen Cocking.

The publishers would like to thank the following for permission to reproduce photographs:

Barnaby's Picture Library, Camera Press, The Consumers' Association, Thames Water Authority (Vales Division), Thames Valley Police Crime Prevention Department, The Samaritans.

The publishers would also like to thank the following examination boards for permission to include questions from previous examination papers:

Associated Lancashire Schools Examining Board (ALSEB)
East Anglian Examinations Board (EAEB)
East Midland Regional Examinations Board (EMREB)
Middlesex Regional Examining Board (MREB)
Oxford  and Cambridge Schools Examination Board (O & C)
Oxford Delegacy of Local Examinations (O)
Scottish Certificate of Education Examination Board (SCE)
South-East Regional Examinations Board (SEREB)
Southern Regional Examinations Board (SREB)
West Midlands Examinations Board (WMEB)

The author would like to thank Mr Tom Matson for typing the manuscript of the book.

# Contents

## Chapter 9 – Feeding the family

## Chapter 10 – Work and leisure

Chapter 1

# Choosing a home

# Choosing the house

Choosing a home of your own is a very important step. You will probab[ly] live in the house for many years, and paying for it will take quite a lot of your income, whether you buy or rent.

**Points to consider**

The price you can afford to pay will usually be your first consideration. Once you start looking at houses you can afford, you should think about the following points.

1 The size of the house should suit the number of people who will be living in it. If it is too small it will feel overcrowded; if it is too large, the house will be expensive to furnish and to keep warm, and difficult to keep clean.

2 *Cavity walls.* All houses now built have cavity walls, that is, outer walls which consist of two brick walls with an air space of about 5 cm between them. The air in the cavity acts as an insulator, helping to keep cold air and noise out, and warm air in. Older houses may not have cavity walls, so they may feel colder.

3 *Damp proof courses* must also be built into new houses. The damp proof course (d.p.c.) is a layer of slate, felt or other material which does not allow water to pass through it. This is placed on all the brick walls about 20 cm above ground level. It prevents damp from the ground passing through it and rising up into the walls of the house.

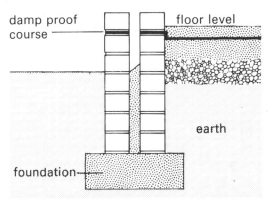

4 Look for signs of damp. Dampness in a house is a serious fault. It is not only unhealthy for the occupants but also leads to the decay of the structure of the house. Stains on the walls suggest that there is no d.p.c. to prevent rising damp, and stains on the upstairs ceilings suggest that the roof is in a bad state of repair. New wallpaper in an old house may be there to cover signs of damp.

5 Examine wooden floors and skirtings. If the wood is soft, damp, or smells musty, there may be wet or dry rot, a fungus which spreads through the timber of the house and is very expensive to treat. Woodworm may also infest timber floors or stairs. Look for small holes in the wood, bored by the woodworm beetle. (See page 86.)

6   *Electrical wiring.* A modern ring circuit system with 13-amp sockets is the safest and most convenient. An older house may need rewiring if you use many electrical appliances. This is expensive.

7   *Plumbing.* Try turning on the taps and flushing the W.C. Consider carefully whether the system for heating the hot water will suit your needs. (See page 50.)

8   *Heating.* A central heating system (page 46) will keep the house warm and comfortable and is more economical to run than separate heaters in every room.

9   *Insulation.* If the house is well insulated and free from draughts you will save fuel while keeping comfortably warm. (See page 54.)

There are many other things you could look for in a house. Is it light and sunny? Are there plenty of cupboards? Is there a garden? Would you like the kitchen/dining-room/living-room combined or separate? Does the house need decorating?

### Solicitor

You will need a solicitor to carry out the legal part of buying a house. He has to be paid for this work, so you must allow for this cost when working out how much money you need in cash.

### Surveyor

When you find a house you like and can afford, it is worth having it checked by a professional surveyor. He will give you a full and detailed report on the structure of the house – the roof, walls, timber and so on. You have to pay him a fee for this, but it could save you hundreds of pounds in the long run.

Questions

1   **What do you consider are the six most important points to look for when choosing a house? Say why each is important.**
2   **What is a damp proof course?**
3   **Why should you check for signs of damp in a house? What signs might you expect to see?**
4   **Sometimes you can choose between a new house in perfect condition and an older house which is much cheaper but needs modernizing. List points for and against each one.**
5   **Explain the work done by (a) a solicitor, (b) a surveyor, when you are buying a house.**

# Renting a home

**Council houses and flats**

Many families live in homes which are rented from the local council o corporation. If you live in a house rented from the council then you are a council tenant. There are several advantages in being a council tenant and in renting rather than buying:

1 The council carries out and pays for all the repairs necessary to keep the house in good order.
2 They pay for modernizations such as installing central heating, though you may have to pay a higher rent after the improvement has been made.
3 You do not have to save a large deposit as you would if you wanted to buy a home.
4 If at any time you have a low income you can apply for a rent rebate so that you pay less rent. Your local council offices, civic centre or town hall will tell you how to do this, and help you to fill in the application form.

However, there are disadvantages, too, in living in rented property:

1 You pay rent all your life, and your home never belongs to you.
2 You may have to wait a long time on the council's housing list. The Local Authority Housing Committee in each area has to decide who has priority on the list. People with families who live in unhealthy, overcrowded conditions, are likely to be given a council house more quickly than a couple who do not have such a particular need.
3 You may not have much choice about the house or the area it is in.
4 You cannot make major alterations without permission.
5 It will probably be difficult to exchange council houses if you decide you want to move.

### Rent book

Whether you rent your home from the council or from a private landlord you should make sure that you are given a rent book. Every time you pay the rent it should be entered in the book and signed by the council rent collector or the landlord. This is your proof that you have paid the rent, so keep the books carefully.

| Date due | Rent | | Total arrears to date | | Date paid | Amount received | | By whom received |
|---|---|---|---|---|---|---|---|---|
| Aug 7 | 12 | 50 | | | Aug 7 | 12 | 50 | P. Jones |
| Aug 14 | 12 | 50 | | | Aug 14 | 12 | 50 | P. Jones |
| Aug 21 | 12 | 50 | | | Aug 21 | 12 | 50 | P. Jones |
| Aug 28 | 12 | 50 | | | Aug 28 | 12 | 50 | P. Jones |
| Sept 4 | 12 | 50 | | | Sept 4 | 12 | 50 | P. Jones |
| Sept 11 | 12 | 50 | | | Sept 11 | 12 | 50 | P. Jones |
| Sept 18 | 12 | 50 | | | Sept 18 | 12 | 50 | P. Jones |
| Sept 25 | 12 | 50 | | | Sept 25 | 12 | 50 | P. Jones |
| Oct 2 | 12 | 50 | | | Oct 2 | 12 | 50 | P. Jones |

## Renting from a private landlord

Houses, flats and bed-sitting rooms can be rented from a private owner or landlord as well as from the council or corporation. They may be furnished or unfurnished. The rents are usually higher than council rents, but again you can apply for help to pay the rent if your income is low. People who live in a privately rented home can apply for a <u>rent allowance</u>, in the same way as people who live in a council house apply for a rent rebate.

When deciding how much rent allowance or rent rebate you are entitled to, the council takes into account your income, your rent, certain other necessary family expenses and the number of people in the family.

It is worth finding out if you can claim by asking at your local town hall, civic centre or housing office. All enquiries are treated in confidence and arrangements are made privately between you and the council.

*How do you find a flat or room to let from a private landlord?*
There are several ways of doing this:

1  You can look in the local paper in the section advertising 'Apartments and Flats to Let'. This is usually the best source.

### 90 Apartments and Flats to Let

**SECOND GIRL** Required to share modern house, own room, all amenities, £32.50 per calendar month (two months in advance). Tel. 864695 after 6.30 p.m.

**SELF CATERING** Accommodation with excellent facilities, professional gentleman only, short lets considered. Whitley Bay 530172.

**HOUSES,** Flats. Bedsitters to let. Contact North East Accomm. Bureau, 11a, Haymarket. Tel. 22666.

**FURNISHED FLAT** for single person, own bedroom, one other gentleman. Felton. Telephone Felton 433.

**YOUNG MAN,** professional, wanted to share large furnished house, own room. Tel. Low Fell 871628.

**BEDSITTER,** just modernised, for young lady, in pleasant part of Jesmond. Tel. 816813.

**WHITLEY BAY.** Two bedroomed furnished flat to let. Must have 3 sharing. Tel. Whitley Bay 523423.

2  You could use the same paper to advertise yourself in the 'Flats and Apartments wanted' column.
3  Some newsagents' shops have postcards in the window showing rooms and flats to let or wanted in that area.

---

### Questions

1  **Who owns council houses and flats?**
2  **What is a council tenant?**
3  **What do you think are the two main advantages of living in council property?**
4  **What do you think are the two main disadvantages of living in council property?**
5  **If you wanted to apply for a rent rebate or rent allowance, where would you go for information on how to do this?**
6  **From whom can you rent flats, apart from the council?**
7  **How would you start to look for a furnished flat?**

# Finding somewhere to live

Sometimes young people have to move away from home because of their work, to go on a training course or to study, and they have to find somewhere to live. They cannot normally have a council flat or buy a house, but there are several possible kinds of accommodation.

### A flat or a bed-sitting room

You may be able to find a furnished flat or room. If you have moved to a new town where you do not know anyone, this could be very lonely, but it could be a suitable first home for a young couple.

Sometimes there may be arguments with the landlord from whom you rent the flat about noise, notice to leave or the amount of rent you pay. Obviously it is best if things can be sorted out agreeably between you and the landlord, but if this is not possible, the <u>rent tribunal</u> may help.

The rent tribunal is there to consider disagreements between landlords and their tenants. They will fix a <u>fair rent</u> for a flat or room and the landlord cannot increase it. They will protect a tenant if a landlord tries to evict him unfairly. The tenant, of course, is expected to act reasonably, by paying his rent regularly, keeping the property in good order and not being too noisy. You can find the address of the rent tribunal in the phone book.

The <u>rent officer</u> sets a fair rent when the flat or house is unfurnished. His address, too, is in the phone book.

## Sharing a flat

Sharing with friends means that you have the company of other young people, and you share costs. The only trouble here is that arguments can easily arise about sharing jobs like cleaning, cooking, or washing up. Sometimes it is difficult to share costs fairly. One person may use more heat and hot water, eat more food, or make more telephone calls than the others, and this can cause resentment if everyone is paying an equal amount.

## Lodgings

You can look in the paper for advertisements for board and lodgings. The landlady cooks meals, keeps your room clean, and provides and washes sheets and pillow-cases. This has several advantages. It saves you the trouble of cooking, cleaning and shopping for food, and makes sure (if the landlady is a good cook) that you are well fed. You usually have the company of other people in the house.

However, you will probably have to pay more each week and will be less independent than you would be in your own flat. You will be less able to please yourself about the hours at which you come in and go out, or the friends who come to visit you.

## Hostels

Some towns and cities have hostels for young people, such as the Y.M.C.A. or Y.W.C.A. If you can get a room in a hostel, which is not always easy, you will have a room, heating, hot water and hot meals provided, plus the company of others. Colleges and universities often have hostels or halls of residence where their own students can live. Charges are fairly high, but everything you need is provided. You can find out about hostels in any area by inquiring at the Citizens' Advice Bureau, or sometimes the local library.

---

### Questions

1 **Name four different kinds of accommodation which could suit someone leaving home for the first time.**
2 **Describe the work of a rent tribunal.**
3 **What is the work of a rent officer?**
4 **Give three advantages of sharing a flat with friends.**
5 **Give three disadvantages.**
6 **How would you find lodgings in a town you did not know?**
7 **List the services you would expect to be provided in lodgings.**
8 **What are the drawbacks of living in lodgings?**
9 **List points for and against living in a hostel.**
10 **What kind of accommodation would suit:**
a **an apprentice on a training course for three months?**
b **a girl going to college in a town where she did not know anyone?**
c **a young couple moving to a town for one year, while the husband was studying?**

# Buying a home

You might decide that you would like to save up to buy a house or flat of your own, rather than rent one. There are several advantages in doing this if it is possible:

1   You have a wider choice of houses, depending, of course, on what you can afford.
2   You can choose the area you would like.
3   If you improve the house, for example by adding central heating, you will increase the value of the house for when you sell it.
4   You don't have to ask the council's permission to make alterations to the house, though you do need planning permission for major alterations or extensions.
5   If you have to move house, you can usually sell the house for more than you paid for it, because house prices are always increasing.
6   Once you have paid for the house (though it may take 25 years or more to do this) it belongs to you. This means that when you are old and have a smaller income, you will not have any further payment to make for the house.

**How do you start to find a house to buy?**

You can:

a   Ask an estate agent to find you a suitable house.
b   Look in the area you have chosen for 'For Sale' notices.
c   Look in the newspapers for 'Houses for Sale' advertisements.

*Reading advertisements*
Certain abbreviations are often found in advertisements:

| | |
|---|---|
| SEMI. | semi-detached |
| C.H. | central heating |
| V.P. | vacant possession |
| W.C. | water closet |
| SEP. W.C. | separate toilet (not in bathroom) |
| 2 REC | 2 living-rooms |
| R.V. | rateable value |
| S.S. | stainless steel |

**COWLEY**

2 Bedrooms
Lounge
Kitchen
Bathroom
Garage
Garden

**Well Appointed**          **£22950**

**For Sale**          **Vernon & Son**

### The area the house is in

Ask yourself some of these questions to help you decide whether the area will be enjoyable to live in.

1 Is it a pleasant area with fields, parks and open spaces, or is it very built up?
2 Is it near the place you work, and the children's schools?
3 Are there good shopping facilities?
4 Is there a good public transport system?
5 Are there a doctor, a dentist, a church and a library nearby?
6 What facilities for entertainment are there, e.g. cinemas, clubs?
7 Are there factories, gas works, a sewage works, a canal, a busy main road or an airport near the house?

Questions

1 **What do you think are the three main advantages of buying a house rather than renting one?**
2 **Make a list of all the good points you would look for in an area you were thinking of moving into.**
3 **List as many things as you can think of that you would rather not have in the area you lived in.**
4 **Cut some 'Property for Sale' columns out of your local paper.**
   **See if you can find out the average cost of:**
a **a 3-bedroomed semi in your area.**
b **a 3-bedroomed terraced house.**
c **a 4-bedroomed detached house.**
d **a 2-bedroomed bungalow.**

# Paying for the house

**Building Societies**

Very few people can save enough money to buy a house outright, as it will cost several thousand pounds. Most people have to borrow most of the money. Often they borrow it from a Building Society.

The Building Society usually lends about 90% of the price of a new house, so if the house costs £20000 they may lend you £18000.

You would have to save up the extra £2000 in cash. This is your deposit.

*Saving for the deposit*

You should start saving a regular amount, weekly or monthly, by putting it into a Building Society account. They will pay you about 10% interest per year for the money you save with them. So if you have saved £100 in your Building Society account you will receive £10 a year from them.

*How the Building Society works*

The Building Society uses this money which people invest (or save) with them to lend out to other people to buy houses.

The Building Society does not lend out money for nothing. You have to pay them back not only the money you borrowed but also interest of about 15%.

**Building Society**
(Keeps 5% for its own expenses.)

Some people save (or invest) their money in a Building Society. They receive about 10% interest for this.

The Building Society lends this money out to other people to buy houses. They charge these people about 15% interest.

*Repayment*

You will have to pay back the loan and the interest over about 25 years, paying a certain amount each month. You do not own the house yourself until you have repaid all the loan.

*Mortgage*

The mortgage is the deed you sign, with details of your agreement.

*Other sources of loans*

Although Building Societies are the main source of borrowing money to buy houses, there are other sources too.

The High Street banks (Lloyds, Midland, Barclay and National Westminster) The banks now lend money for mortgages, offering similar terms and conditions to the building societies. Your bank manager would arrange this.

Local authorities may offer money for mortgages, especially for older properties in their own area. If the house you want to buy is an older one, for example built before 1919, you may find that your local authority is more willing to lend you money to buy it than a Building Society is.

Insurance companies may also arrange a loan to buy a house.

**Who can ask for a loan?**

Women as well as men can apply for a loan. Naturally the Building Society will not lend money to just anybody who asks for it.

1  They are more likely to lend you money if you save with them.
2  They will check that you have a steady income so that they know you will be able to pay them back.
3  They usually lend $2\frac{1}{2}$ to 3 times your yearly salary. Sometimes a Building Society will take a married woman's salary into account as well as her husband's.
4  They will check the condition of the house. They are less likely to lend money for a house that is either very old or in a poor neighbourhood.
5  First-time buyers may be given priority.

Questions

1  **What percentage of the price of a new house can you usually borrow from a Building Society?**
2  **What is the deposit?**
3  **How should you save for the deposit on a house?**
4  **What does the Building Society do with the money people save with them?**
5  **Draw the diagram to show how the Building Society works.**
6  **How long does it usually take to pay off the mortgage on a house?**
7  **How often do you make mortgage repayments?**
8  **What is a mortgage?**
9  **What information will a Building Society require before they decide whether to lend money?**
10 **How much could you expect to borrow if you earned £4000 a year?**

# Rates

## Who pays rates?

Every householder pays rates to the local council. If you live in a rented home your rates are usually included in your rent. If you are buying your own home you will have to pay rates as well as the mortgage.

### What does the council do with the rates?

The local authority, or council, uses the money collected in rates to pay for local services which everyone in the area uses, for example:

collecting refuse
disposal of sewage
building and repairing roads
schools, libraries, clinics, swimming pools, youth clubs, parks
the Fire Service and the Police

---

**WEST OXFORDSHIRE DISTRICT COUNCIL**
TREASURER'S DEPARTMENT
26, CHURCH GREEN
WITNEY, OXON.
Tel. Witney 2941

## RATE ACCOUNT 1977-78

The District Council have made a General Rate together with additional items for certain Parishes in respect of the year 1st April 77 to 31st March 78. The Rate shall become due on the 1st April 77 but may be paid in two equal instalments. Full details of the Rate are shown on the enclosed leaflet with other information. This account must be produced to the Chief Income Officer when any enquiry is made.

Date

01/04/77

MR PAUL SOUSTER
7 TRISTRAM ROAD
DUCKLINGTON
WITNEY OXON

or Occupier

Assessment No.

326 311300702X

| Description/Situation | Rateable Value £ | Rate Code (see overleaf) |
|---|---|---|
| HOUSE & GARAGE 7 TRISTRAM ROAD DUCKLINGTON | 204 | 2 |

Amount £

| Period (inclusive) From | To | General Rate £ | Water Rate £ | Gen. Services Charge £ | |
|---|---|---|---|---|---|
| 01/04/77 | 31/03/78 | 123.01 | 14.89 | 18.21 | 156.11 |

AMOUNT DUE FOR YEAR        156.11

TOTAL AMOUNT DUE        156.11

RECEIPTING SPACE

The account includes the Water Rate and General Services Charge which the Council are authorised to collect on behalf of the Thames Water Authority.

Neil J. B. Robson, A.C.A., F.R.V.A., A.M.B.I.M.
*Treasurer of the Council*

## How much do you pay?

The amount you pay in rates depends on the rateable value of your house. The rateable value (r.v.) is related to the value of your house.

The more amenities the home has (gardens, garage, central heating, number of rooms, the area it is in) the higher the rateable value and the more you pay in rates.

Rates are assessed at so much in the pound. If the rates one year are 80p in the £ and the rateable value of your house is £200, your yearly rates bill will be $200 \times 80p = £160.00$.

### When do you pay?

Rates are normally paid every half-year, though you may arrange to pay each month instead if you prefer.

### Rate rebates

If you have an average or low income you may be entitled to a rate rebate. You apply to your local council for this and they may reduce the amount you pay, according to your income and your family expenses.

### Water rates

All householders have to pay a water rate as well as the general rate. This money is used to provide us with a clean water supply and for other services, including the prevention of pollution of our rivers and seas.

## Government grants

Standard grants are available from the government to improve older houses which do not have these basic amenities:

indoor W.C.
bath or shower
sink
wash basin
hot and cold water supply

Other grants are available for major alterations and modernizations. Your local council will give you advice on how to apply for these.

---

Questions

1 **Who has to pay rates?**
2 **How do council tenants pay their rates?**
3 **How often do you pay the rates if you are buying your own home?**
4 **List some of the more important services to the community which are paid for by the rates.**
5 **The rateable value of your house is £240. The rates are 90p in the £. How much will your yearly rates bill be? How much would you have to pay each month?**
6 **The rateable value of your house is £200. The rates are £1.20p in the £. How much will your yearly rates bill be?**
7 **Who can apply for a rate rebate?**
8 **Name two services paid for by the water rates.**

# Further work on chapter 1

1   (a) **A young couple is thinking about buying their first home. Name two sources they could consult for information about homes for sale.**
    **(b) Briefly say what you understand by each of the following terms: a bungalow, a high-rise flat, a semi-detached house, a terraced house.**
    **(c) Name three other professional people you would consult during the purchase of your home.** (EMREB)

2   **Describe as many ways as you can in which the local authority, or council, can give you advice or financial help in matters related to your home.**

3   (a) **The following advertisement appeared in a local newspaper: A 3-bedroomed semi, oil c.h., bathroom, sep. W.C., hall, lounge, dining-room, fitted kitchen s/s sink, gardens front and rear, r.v. £100, £25 000 o.n.o.**
    **Explain the following abbreviations: semi, c.h., sep. W.C., s/s sink, r.v., o.n.o.**
    **(b) What do the following mean? (i) general rate (ii) rateable value. How is the rateable value of property arrived at?** (ASLEB)

4   **Explain in your own words what a Building Society is and how it works. Name some Building Societies in your area. Find out the current interest rate charged on mortgages and the current rate paid to investors.**

5   **Write notes on each of the following terms: (a) tenant, (b) rent allowance, (c) rent rebate, (d) mortgage, (e) rateable value, (f) standard grant, (g) fair rent, (h) rate rebate.**

6   (a) **Write a paragraph each about the work of three of the following: Rent Tribunals; Local Authority Housing Committee; estate agents; Building Societies.**
    **(b) List the ways in which you could find accommodation to rent.**
    **(c) What kind of accommodation would you like? Give reasons.** (O)

---

**Books for further reading**

*Science for Housecraft* **John Robinson** Edward Arnold
*At Home with Science* **O. F. G. Kilgour** Heinemann Educational
*Hygiene in the Home* **Elisabeth Norton** Mills and Boon
*Running a Home is Fun* **Good Housekeeping** Ebury Press
*Homecraft* **Margaret Clark** Routledge and Kegan Paul

# Chapter 2
# Services to the home

# Gas

### Where does gas come from?

*The North Sea (natural gas)*

A lot of the gas now used in this country comes from the bed of the North Sea. The gas is piped in from the sea and is stored near the coast in large containers. From there, it goes in pipes under the streets to houses and factories.

*Coal gas (or town gas)*

This is a gas which is given off from coal, when it is heated in large closed ovens. It is stored in gas holders and distributed around the town in pipes below the ground.

Gas holder

### The safe use of gas

Remember that gas burns easily and is highly explosive. Be very careful when using gas, and always follow these rules:

*Buying*
Buy gas appliances with one or both of these labels:

British Standards Institution
safety mark

British Standards Institution
Kitemark

*Installing*
Have all gas appliances installed by a qualified fitter. The gas board have lists of 'C.O.R.G.I.' fitters in your area whom they recommend as being competent installers.

*Using*
Only use gas appliances in rooms with an adequate supply of fresh air. When gas burns it gives off carbon monoxide fumes which are poisonous. If the room does not have adequate ventilation, dangerous amounts of carbon monoxide gather in the room. This causes drowsiness and has even caused death in some cases.

*Servicing*
To make sure that gas appliances work safely and efficiently they should be serviced every two years or so, especially gas fires and central heating boilers. Again, the gas board will arrange this for you.

*Leakage*
If you suspect a gas leak, turn the gas off at once at the main tap in the house, and call the gas board, who operate a 24-hour emergency service.
Never look for a gas leak with the naked flame of a candle or a match; if you did, you could cause an explosion.

---

### Questions

1 **Where does much of the natural gas used in this country come from?**
2 **What is town gas made from?**
3 **How is gas distributed to houses and factories where it is required?**
4 **You want to change the position of the cooker in your kitchen. How would you find a gas fitter who was competent to do this?**
5 **How would you provide adequate ventilation when using a gas fire in your living-room? Why is it necessary to do this?**
6 **You come home one afternoon and there is a strong smell of gas in the house. Describe exactly what you would do.**

# The gas meter

Gas is measured, at present, in cubic feet. The amount used in a house is measured on the gas meter, which often looks like this:

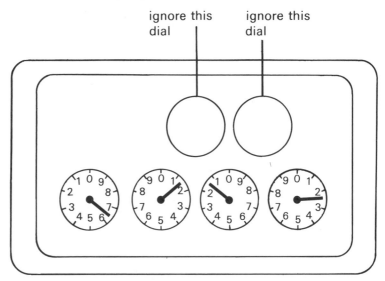

The reading on this meter is 6112.

### How to read the gas meter

1   Ignore the two top dials.
2   Working from left to right, write down the smaller of the two figures between which the hand is pointing.
3   If the hand lies between 0 and 1 the smaller figure will be 0. If the hand lies between 9 and 0 the smaller figure will be 9.
4   When you have your 4-figure reading, add 00 after the reading. This is now your meter reading in cubic feet. The meter shown above therefore reads 611200.
5   Take away your last meter reading from this meter reading to find how many cubic feet of gas you have used since the last time your meter was read. Your gas bill will be based on the number of cubic feet you have used.

### *Newer Meters*

Some meters have a direct reading index which shows all the figures in a line, like this:

| 6 | 1 | 1 | 2 | 0 | 0 |
|---|---|---|---|---|---|

In some new houses, gas and electricity meters are outside the house in a locked cupboard, so that the men from the gas and electricity boards can read the meter even if you are out.

Measurement of gas is to be changed from cubic feet to cubic metres, but the method of reading the meter will be the same.

**Payment**

Gas meters are usually read once a quarter (every three months) and bills are sent out to consumers after this.

*Budget scheme*

If you wish you can pay for your gas in equal monthly instalments which are based on the amount of gas you usually use.

This means you can work out how much to allow every month to cover the cost. Your gas board will give you a form to sign if you wish to make use of this budget scheme.

Accounts are settled once a year and if you have under- or over-paid your account, it will be adjusted to allow for this.

Questions

1 **What are the readings on the following gas meters?**

a    497500

b    838400

c    165900

2 **How often are gas meters usually read and bills sent out to the consumer?**

3 **List the advantages of paying for your gas through a monthly budget scheme.**

# Electricity in the home

### Using electricity safely

It would be hard to imagine life at home without electricity for lighting, heating, cooking, television and many other things.

But as well as being useful, electricity can also be dangerous. It can cause accidents and even death. All electrical appliances must be used properly and looked after carefully. You should make sure that everyone in your family follows these safety rules:

1 Never let water come into contact with electrical current. The combination of water and electricity is very dangerous. Do not let plugs or appliances become damp, or handle them with wet hands.

2 Avoid using adaptors if possible, and certainly do not overload them by plugging lots of appliances into them.

3 Only use good quality plugs that conform to British Standards.

4 Keep electrical equipment in good condition and do not use it if any of the wires or cords are frayed.

5 Do not attempt electrical repairs or wiring yourself. Your electricity board will have a list of expert electrical contractors in your area.

6 Make sure plugs are wired correctly and are fitted with the right size fuse (see below). Only wire plugs and mend fuses yourself if you know exactly what you are doing.

7 Look for the B.E.A.B. (British Electrotechnical Approvals Board) mark of safety on every electrical appliance you buy. Avoid buying second-hand appliances.

B.E.A.B. mark of safety

8 Special care is needed in the bathroom which can become damp and steamy.

a Socket outlets are not allowed in bathrooms except special shaver sockets.

b You must never carry any portable appliance (except a shaver) into the bathroom, even if it is plugged in outside. This includes hair-driers, electric fires, record players, heated rollers and so on. Ignoring this safety rule can cause fatal accidents.

c The light should be operated by a pull-cord switch.

d The radiant heaters made for bathrooms must be permanently fixed and wired to the wall, out of reach from the bath or shower, and operated by a pull-cord.

### Plugs – fuses – earthing

*How to wire a modern fused plug*
Remember – The new colours are:
Green/Yellow to Earth
Brown        to Live
Blue         to Neutral

The old colours were:
Green to Earth
Red    to Live
Black  to Neutral

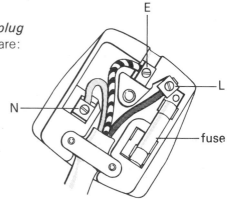

#### Fuses

Electric current is carried around the house through wires specially laid for it. Fuses are just wires with a low melting point. They are there as a safety device. If a fault occurs and the current is too great for safety then the fuse will melt and break the circuit (the flow of electricity).

Modern appliances have a fuse within the plug. You should always fit a fuse of the correct size into the plug according to the wattage of the appliance.

Plug fuses are mainly either:
3 amp for most appliances up to 720 watts.
13 amp for most appliances between 720 and 3000 watts.

#### Earthing

Plugs and electrical wiring systems are fitted with an earth wire as a safety precaution.

Normally, the electric current travels along the path prepared for it, that is, along the wires. But if a fault occurs the electricity may leave this path and will instead take the shortest path to earth.

If the plug is fitted with an earth wire, then the current will run down to the earth through this earth wire, and not through the person holding the appliance.

---

### Questions

1 **List five common causes of electrical accidents in the home.**
2 **How can you avoid electrical accidents in the home?**
3 **How would you get in touch with an electrical contractor who could safely rewire your house?**
4 **Why are fuses fitted into plugs and electrical wiring systems?**
5 **Explain how a fuse works.**
6 **What size fuse should you fit into the plug of:**
a **a 200 watt refrigerator**
b **a lamp with a 100 watt bulb**
c **a 1 kW portable electric fire?**
7 **Explain how an earth wire acts as a safety device.**
8 **Look inside the plug of an electrical appliance and see if it is correctly wired up as in the diagram above.**
**Check to see whether it has the correct size of fuse fitted.**

# The supply of electricity

### Volts

Electricity is conducted, or flows, along wires from the generating station to the home. The pressure behind the flow is called the <u>voltage</u>. Supplies to houses in this country are about <u>240 volts</u>.

### Units

The amount of electricity used in any house is measured by the meter. It is measured and paid for by the unit. If you had used 400 units of electricity and electricity cost 4p per unit, the cost to you would be $400 \times 4p = £16$.

### Reading the meter

To find out how many units you have actually used in a quarter (three months) so that you can pay your bill, you read the meter. You then compare this reading with your last meter reading. The difference between the two gives the number of units you have used. The reading on this meter is 72483.

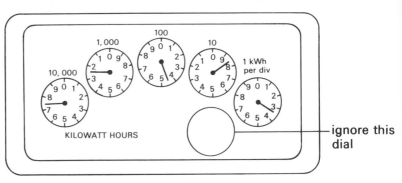

1   As with the gas meter (see page 18), when the hand lies between the two figures you read the smaller figure.
2   If the hand lies between 0 and 1 the smaller figure will be 0.
    If the hand lies between 9 and 0 the smaller figure will be 9.
3   The numbers on the dials are alternately clockwise and anti-clockwise.

#### Newer meters

Sometimes electric meters are simply read as a line of numbers, like some gas meters.

| 7 | 2 | 4 | 8 | 3 |
|---|---|---|---|---|

### The cost of using electricity

Different electrical appliances need different amounts of power to make them work. For example, an electric cooker needs more power than an electric light bulb.

### Watts

The power of electricity is measured in <u>watts</u>. A cooker might need 12 000 watts to function, whereas a light bulb might need only 100 watts. Electrical appliances have their wattage marked on them.

The amount of electricity any appliance uses (and so the amount it costs you to run it) depends on two things:

1   The <u>wattage</u> (that is, the number of watts it uses).
2   The length of time you use it for.

### Kilowatt

1000 watts are called a <u>kilowatt</u> (kW). One kW can be used for one hour for the cost of one unit. Therefore: 1 unit = 1 kilowatt used for 1 hour.

### Kilowatt hour

A kilowatt hour means 1000 watts used for 1 hour.

If electricity costs 4p per unit (that is, per kilowatt hour):
a 1000 watt (1 kW) fire will cost 4p to use for 1 hour.
a 500 watt iron will cost 2p to use for 1 hour.
a 3 kW immersion heater will cost 12p to use for 1 hour.
a 250 watt food mixer will cost 1p to use for 1 hour.

Once you know the current cost of a unit, you can work out how much it will cost you to use any electrical appliance.

### The off-peak rate

The rate for electricity used during the night is about half the usual cost per unit. Off-peak electricity is used for night storage heaters, under-floor or ceiling heating systems and off-peak water heaters.

### Easy payment schemes

These save you having to pay heavy quarterly bills by spreading the cost. The schemes may include:

1   Regular, equal monthly payments.
2   Savings stamps bought from your electricity showroom.
3   Payments made of how much you like, when you like, at the showroom. The amount you pay is deducted from your bill before it is sent to you.

---

### Questions

1   **Explain what these terms mean: (a) voltage, (b) unit.**
2   **How often are electricity bills usually paid?**
3   **Look at the information marked on any three electrical appliances, for example, cooker, food mixer and iron. At what voltage should each be used?**
4   **Your meter reading on 1 June was 84 671. Your meter reading on 1 September is 85 391. If electricity costs 4p per unit, what will be the cost of the units used in this quarter?**
5   **Explain exactly what these terms mean: (a) watts, (b) kilowatt, (c) kilowatt hour.**
6   **What two factors decide how much it will cost to use any electrical appliance?**
7   **Name four electrical appliances and for each state:**
a   **the number of watts it uses.**
b   **how much it would cost to run for 1 hour at 4p a unit.**

# The water supply

In the great majority of houses in this country you can have a constant supply of clean, pure water by simply turning on a tap.

## Paying for the water

A lot of time and effort goes into providing this service, which is organized by local authorities. This service is paid for by the water rates which every householder has to pay, half-yearly. This rate may be paid separately or may be collected in with the general rates.

### Other water services

The water authorities are also responsible for sewage disposal, for the prevention of water pollution, for fisheries and navigation, and for nature conservation and the provision of recreational facilities such as sailing and boating.

## Collecting the water

### Surface water

When rain falls on to hard ground it flows over the surface of the hillsides and forms small streams which flow together to form rivers and lakes.

### Underground water

Some rain sinks down through porous ground until it reaches impermeable rock (which does not allow water to pass through it), then it collects to form large underground rivers and lakes.

### Sources of pure water

Water authorities can collect water from any of these sources. Some sources of water are purer than others. Water is usually collected in large storage reservoirs on high land, or from deep underground lakes where it is likely to be clean and uncontaminated.

### Contamination of water

As they flow farther downstream, rivers often become contaminated, especially near farmland and towns. Farm animals may pollute the water. Chemicals used on farm land, such as pesticides and fertilizers, drain through the soil and into streams and rivers. Factories may allow poisonous waste materials to flow into the rivers untreated.

Obviously it is important to make sure that our drinking water is as pure as possible by collecting it from highland areas or underground lakes.

Before the water is used, the water authorities treat it to make sure it is free from two main types of impurities.

1. It must be free from large objects, such as stones, fish or weed. These are removed by filtering the water through layers of gravel and sand.
2. The water must be free from bacteria which might cause diseases such as typhoid or dysentery. This is done by adding chlorine to the water in carefully measured amounts. Too little will not kill bacteria, too much will leave a taste, as in the swimming baths.

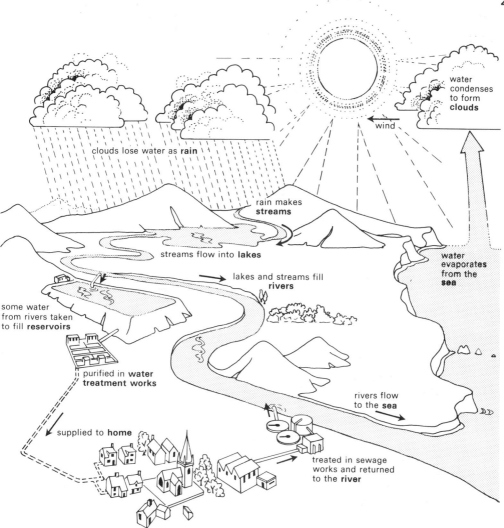

The water cycle

Some local authorities also add <u>fluoride</u> to the water to help prevent tooth decay in children. (See page 173.)

When the water has been fully treated like this it is piped to the town, often many miles away, in large underground pipes, and eventually it reaches your home.

## Questions

1  **Who pays for the provision of a pure water supply, and how often?**
2  **List some of the other services provided by the water authority.**
3  **How are underground rivers and lakes formed?**
4  **Name two sources of water which are likely to be fairly pure.**
5  **Why does river water become more contaminated as it flows downstream?**
6  **Why is water filtered through sand and gravel beds?**
7  **Why are (a) chlorine, and (b) fluoride added to the water supply?**

# Hard and soft water

### What is hard water?

You will know if you live in, or visit, an area supplied with hard water because when you try to wash your hands with soap you will find it difficult to get the soap to make a good lather. You will find scum forming around the wash basin or bath. A hard, chalky deposit called 'fur' will form inside the kettle, and this will make the kettle feel heavy even when it is empty.

*Why does this happen?*

The water is like this basically because it contains mineral salts dissolved in it. When rainwater falls on to certain soils such as limestone or chalk, it sinks through the soil dissolving some of the limestone or chalk as it passes through. When this water is collected from underground and piped to your home, it still contains these dissolved salts. The mineral salts causing hard water are mainly calcium and magnesium bicarbonates and calcium and magnesium sulphates.

### The disadvantages of hard water

1   As it is difficult to produce a lather with hard water, you have to use more soap and more detergents, so it costs you more money.

2   Hard water is much more harsh on your skin and hair. Washing your hair and skin in soft water makes them feel soft and silky.

3   Clothes washed in soft water feel softer to touch, and it is easier to rinse soap powders or detergents away. Most washing powders and liquids now have water softeners added to them, to make washing easier for people in hard water areas.

4   Hard water causes the inside of the kettle to 'fur up'. When you put the kettle on to heat water you have to heat the chalky layer as well as the water, so it will take longer and use more fuel. You can buy preparations from a hardware shop which will remove the fur quite easily.

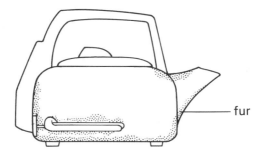
fur

5   The boiler and pipes can fur up, sometimes causing a complete blockage. This is more difficult and more expensive to remove than the fur in a kettle.

6   Scum will form around the edge of the bath or wash basins when you try to wash with soap. It is unpleasant in appearance and makes the bath harder to clean.

## The two types of hard water

The mineral salts causing hard water are mainly calcium bicarbonate, magnesium bicarbonate, calcium sulphate and magnesium sulphate.

### Temporary hard water

This contains calcium and magnesium bicarbonates. This water can be softened by boiling. When the water is heated these salts change to chalk. As this is not soluble in water the chalk falls as a deposit. This is not serious in the kettle and can quite easily be removed, but hot water boilers and pipes can become so furred inside that they get completely blocked.

If you live in an area where the water is very hard you will need to have the deposit cleared from the pipes and boiler every few years.

### Permanent hard water

This contains calcium and magnesium sulphates. It cannot be softened by boiling but it can be softened by adding washing soda (sodium carbonate), borax or bath salts to your washing water. These change the dissolved salts into a fine powder, so that the water itself is left soft.

## A water softening system

If you live in an area where the water is very hard and causes you a lot of inconvenience, it may be worth installing a rather expensive water softening system, which works using a resin such as permutite.

This system softens all the water as it enters the house, so it prevents the furring of pipes as well as providing soft water for washing. It works in the following way. All the water coming into the house passes through a container full of the resin, and is softened by it before passing through the pipes in the house. After a while the resin becomes exhausted and has to be recharged with a solution of ordinary salt.

---

Questions

1  **List all the points by which a householder would realize he was living in a hard water area.**
2  **Outline in your own words how hard water is caused.**
3  **Imagine you live in an area where the water is very hard. Describe what you consider are the three main disadvantages of your water supply.**
4  **How do detergent manufacturers help people in hard water areas when they make their products?**
5  **What are the mineral salts which cause temporary hard water?**
6  **How can temporary hard water be softened?**
7  **When a kettle of temporary hard water is boiled, what happens to the salts dissolved in the water?**
8  **What are the mineral salts which cause permanent hard water?**
9  **Name three products which will soften this water.**
10  **Describe how these products soften the water.**
11  **What is the advantage of having water softening equipment installed in your house rather than just softening the water as you use it?**
12  **Explain how this type of water softening system works.**

# The removal of liquid waste

Household waste can be divided into two types, liquid waste and dry waste. The local authority is responsible for disposing of this waste. They pay for this with money from the rates.

Years ago, before there was organized refuse collection and main drains and sewers, people in towns and cities often had no way of disposing of their refuse except by throwing it into the streets. This made the streets smell unpleasant, and encouraged the spread of rats, flies and other pests and disease-carrying bacteria.

### The disposal of liquid waste: drainage

Three types of liquid waste have to be disposed of from the home:
1   Waste from the lavatory.
2   Household water from the sink, bath and wash basin.
3   Storm water (rain water which falls on the roof).

#### Waste from the lavatory

When the W.C. is flushed, the water forces away the contents, leaving clean water in the S-bend at the bottom of the pan. This water prevents smells and insects from the drains coming back up the pipes into the house.

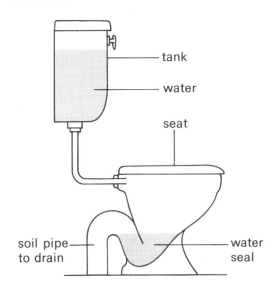

The pipe from the W.C. is a wide pipe to allow for the efficient flushing away of all waste matter. It leads into a vertical <u>soil pipe</u>. The top of the soil pipe is open for ventilation and must extend above the level of the roof. It leads down below the ground, enclosed all the time, and then to the main drains which run under the street.

Between the house and the main sewer under the street, there is an <u>inspection chamber</u> covered with an iron manhole cover. This allows access to the drains if it is necessary.

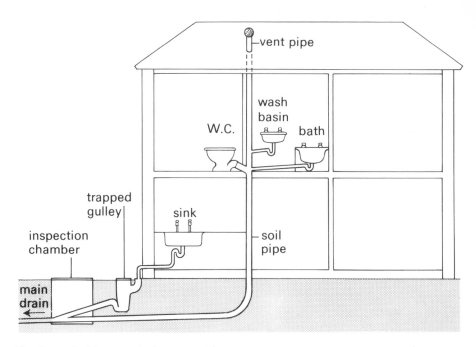

The household water drainage system

### Water from sink, bath and wash basin

This water can be drained away in narrower pipes than those from the W.C. Below all sinks and wash basins there is a U-bend in the pipe which is always full of water. This stops smells coming up from the drains and is useful if pipes become blocked. There is a plug or 'cleaning eye' at the base which can be undone to empty the trap, so that any blockage can be easily removed.

In modern houses, the water from the wash basin and bath joins the soil pipe and leads to the main sewer. Waste water from the kitchen sink runs straight down a pipe into an open drain outside.

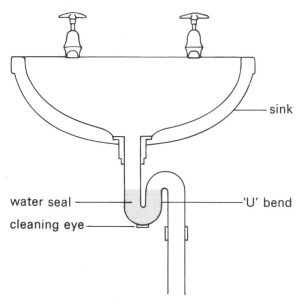

### Storm water

In order to help keep the home dry, the rain falling on to the roof of the house is collected in gutters and runs down pipes on the outside wall of the house into an open drain. This either then goes to the main sewer under the street, or, as it is quite clean and harmless, it is sometimes just drained away into the soil.

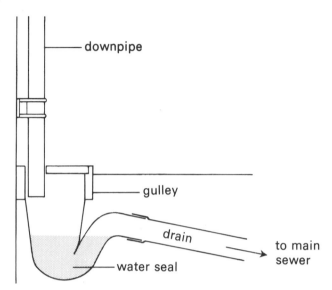

## Keeping the drainage system clean and hygienic

As all parts of the drainage system are concerned with removing waste matter which may contain millions of bacteria it is obviously important to keep them as clean and fresh-smelling as possible.

### The W.C.

The W.C. must be kept clean and hygienic to prevent the spread of the bacteria present in human excreta which cause sickness and disease.

1  The lavatory pan can be kept clean with a specially shaped brush kept only for this purpose.
2  Special powder or liquid cleaners containing bleach can be used in the pan.
3  The lavatory seat and the handles of the cistern and door must be regularly disinfected as bacteria are likely to be transferred on to them from people's hands.
4  Hands must be washed after every visit to the lavatory. Children should be trained to do this.

### The sink

The sink must be carefully cleaned after use to keep it free from particles of food and grease.

1  After washing up, the sink and draining board should be washed down with hot soapy water.
2  Clean water should be run through the sink to make sure that the water in the U-bend is fresh and clean.
3  A few drops of disinfectant can be put down the sink daily to prevent bacterial growth.

### Blocked sinks

Sometimes a sink becomes blocked and the water runs away very slowly, or not at all. If this happens you can take the following action:

1 Remove any pieces of food which may be blocking the sink outlet.
2 Use a plunger vigorously over the outlet, and try to dislodge the blockage.

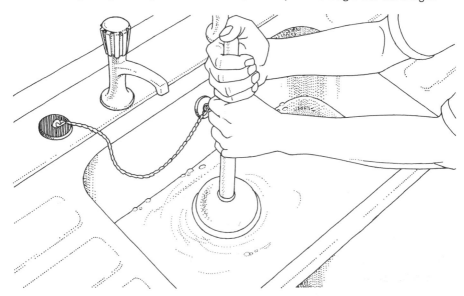

3 If this does not work, you can unscrew the plug under the U-bend below the sink and you may find the cause of the blockage. Remember that the water in the U-bend will come out when you do this, so be sure to have a bucket ready to catch it.
4 Caustic soda crystals can be put down the drain. This will clear most blockages, but it must be used with extreme caution as it can cause severe burns to the skin.
5 If all these measures fail, you will have to call a plumber, or a commercial firm specializing in unblocking pipes and drains.

### Outside drains

Remove litter and leaves from the drain regularly. Pour a hot solution of soda water or disinfectant down once a week, to prevent smells.

---

### Questions

1 **What are the three types of liquid waste which have to be removed from the home?**
2 **Describe how waste is removed from the W.C., illustrating your answer with a diagram.**
3 **Draw a diagram to show the U-bend below a sink or wash basin. Explain why it is there.**
4 **How and why should the W.C. be cleaned daily?**
5 **When washing up after a meal, how should you clean the sink?**
6 **How can you prevent your sink becoming blocked? What could you do to clear a blockage?**

# Sewage disposal

Once the liquid waste leaves the drains of each house it passes into the sewers under the street leading to the sewage works.

When it gets there it has to be treated to make it harmless. The harmful bacteria in the sewage have to be destroyed and this is done slowly by the natural action of other bacteria and air on the sewage.

The sewage flows into tanks where bacteria begin to break it down. The sludge, or more solid matter, gradually sinks to the bottom of the tank and separates from the liquid.

The sludge is removed and further treated by bacteria to make it harmless. It is dried and rotted and can be sold as fertilizer provided it does not contain harmful chemical waste from factories.

The liquid is acted upon further by bacteria in the air, until it becomes harmless. Then it is allowed to flow into rivers.

Sewage works

## Chemical pollution

Although these processes make the sewage free from harmful bacteria, they cannot always treat chemical substances which may have entered the waste. The Water Authorities make a constant effort to keep our rivers and seas free from pollution.

You can sometimes see froth floating on rivers; this may come from detergents which could not be broken down by the processes in the sewage works. Manufacturers of washing powders now produce detergents which are 'biodegradable' and can be broken down and made harmless by natural biological action. All British detergents for domestic use are biodegradable, although detergents used in industry may still cause pollution.

## Septic tanks and cesspits

Some houses in country areas are not connected to the main drains and sewers. Their waste is normally drained to a septic tank or a cesspit.

### Septic tanks

Septic tanks normally consist of two pits below ground level. The sewage drains from the house into the first tank where bacterial action slowly breaks the sewage down to a more liquid form. The heavier part of the liquid, or sludge, gradually sinks to the bottom of the tank and is later removed by the local authority. The liquid part passes into the second pit where further bacterial action slowly makes it harmless. After this has happened, the clean effluent is drained away into the ground.

### Cesspits

A cesspit is a pit below the ground, situated well away from the house. It must be watertight, ventilated and have a removable cover for emptying. All the sewage from the house is drained into the pit which is emptied when necessary by the local authority. A suction hose drains the sewage into a covered cart similar to the type used for cleaning street drains. It is then taken to the nearest sewage works for treatment.

---

## Questions

1  **Explain briefly how sewage is treated to make it harmless.**
2  **How are the solid and liquid parts of sewage disposed of after they have been treated?**
3  **What is a 'biodegradable' detergent?**
4  **Describe two ways of disposing of sewage hygienically in households which are not connected to main drains.**

# The removal of household refuse

### Dustbins

The contents of a householder's dustbin may include a variety of materials, including broken glass and china, food, peelings, paper, plastic and ashes. Garden rubbish should not be put into the bin. It should either be burned or rotted down in a compost heap and then used to enrich the soil.

Dustbins may be made of various materials:
1 *Galvanized metal bins.* These are hardwearing but noisy. The lids may be metal, but are sometimes made of plastic or rubber, which are much quieter in use.
2 *Plastic bins.* These are lighter and less noisy, but you cannot put hot ashes into them.
3 *Plastic or paper sacks,* in wire mesh containers, are used in some areas. The whole bag is removed and replaced by a new one once a week. This method is clean, but the bags are easy to damage.

### Care of the bin

It is important to keep the dustbin as clean and hygienic as you can, because otherwise it makes an ideal place for bacteria and flies to breed.

You should follow all these rules:
1 Make sure the lid fits firmly, to keep out flies, vermin (rats and mice), dogs and cats.
2 Wrap all damp waste such as vegetable peelings in paper before putting them into the bin, or they will stick to its sides.
3 Wash tins before putting them into the bin. Do not put other rubbish inside them, as tins are often removed by magnets later and sold as scrap metal.
4 Stand the dustbin on bricks to help ventilate it.
5 Scrub the bin out regularly with disinfectant. Allow it to dry before re-using it.
6 Line the bottom of the bin with thick layers of newspaper before putting refuse in, to help keep it clean.

## Paper salvage

If you have a lot of clean paper and card, put it out separately from the rest of your rubbish, as many local authorities can sell clean paper for recycling.

## Rubbish chutes

Large blocks of flats normally have a central rubbish chute with an opening in or near each kitchen. The refuse goes down the chute into very large bins which are emptied into dustcarts fitted with mechanical lifting devices.

## Waste disposal units

Some sinks have a waste disposal unit fitted underneath them. Most waste, including bones and broken china but excluding cans, string and cloth, can be put into them. Electrically driven knives grind it to a fine pulp and it is washed away down the sink. It is a simple and hygienic way of disposing of refuse, but can be expensive to buy and install.

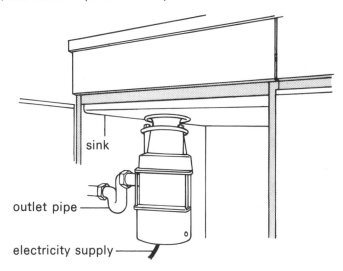

### *Safety*

It is important to choose a waste disposal unit which will be safe in use. The safest kind will only work when the guard lid is in position. This avoids the possibility of children putting not only rubbish but also their hands on to the sharp blades. The electrical on/off switch should always be positioned out of reach of children.

---

Questions

1 **What are the advantages and disadvantages of the different types of dustbins you can use?**
2 **How would you keep a plastic dustbin clean?**
3 **Describe how a waste disposal unit works.**

# Refuse disposal

The disposal of the contents of the householders' bins is organized by the local authority and is paid for from the rates. They may dispose of the waste in various ways:

### Dumping at sea

Towns near the coast may dump rubbish in the sea, far enough out to prevent it being washed back on to the beaches.

### Rubbish tips or dumps

In some areas, all the rubbish is tipped into large pits in the ground. It may be burned, and then covered with a layer of earth, until the pit is filled. When one is full another pit is used.

Although this method of disposal is simple and cheap, it is not very satisfactory. The rubbish may be blown around by the wind, and it can smell unpleasant and attract rats and flies looking for food. It is, however, a method quite widely used in country areas where there is more space to situate the tip away from houses.

Rubbish tip

### Refuse disposal plants

The most modern plants will sort mechanically from the refuse any materials which can be sold.

The money obtained from selling the refuse helps to keep the cost of operating the service as low as possible, and so this both prevents waste and saves money for the ratepayer.

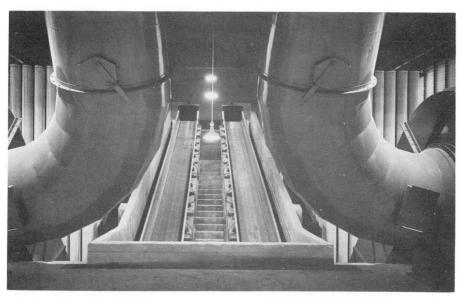

Modern refuse disposal plant

### Materials which can be salvaged

These vary, according to the mechanical equipment installed at the plant. A modern 'reclamation plant' could salvage some of the following:

1  Some metals, for example tin cans, can be removed by magnets.
2  Paper and plastics can be formed into pellets and sold as industrial fuel.
3  Items which cannot be burned, such as pieces of concrete or broken china, can be used for filling in land which is being prepared for building sites, or after quarrying.
4  Ashes produced after burning waste can be used by farmers on the land.
5  Some refuse disposal plants can use the heat from their incinerators to provide their own heating.
6  In some plants the heat may be used to work electric generators, but this is not often economic.

Questions

1  **List some of the ways in which local authorities dispose of the rubbish from dustbins. What are (a) the advantages, and (b) the disadvantages of each method?**
2  **Who pays for the disposal of refuse?**
3  **Name four of the materials which can be salvaged from household rubbish for sale or re-use.**

# Further work on chapter 2

1  Find out how gas is produced from coal. Describe the many by-products from the coal gas industry which are in everyday use.

2  Some natural gas is brought to this country from North Africa. Write an account of how it is brought here and draw a map to show what route it takes, from the Sahara to the major cities in England.

3  You may have used Calor gas heaters or cookers when on holiday. There are also models available for use in the home. Find out:
(a) where they can be bought and how much they cost.
(b) the price of a cylinder of gas and how long it could last.
(c) the advantages and disadvantages of a Calor gas fire or cooker in the home.

4  Explain:
(a) the precaution you would take in using, cleaning and repairing electrical apparatus.
(b) the purpose and action of (i) a fuse wire and (ii) a three-pin plug.
(O & C)

5  An electric iron is marked with the following information. Explain the meaning of each:
(a) Volts  225–250
(b) Watts 1000

6  Ask at your local electricity showrooms for a leaflet describing the various tariffs available for domestic users. Give an account of each one and describe a household for which each would be economical.

7  Make a list of the major electrical appliances in your home and their wattages. Look at an old electricity bill and note how many units you used in the quarter. Notice the price of the first units and the price of any subsequent units. Check to see if there are any extra charges and that you understand how the total charge is arrived at.

   If you intended to change to equal monthly payments, how much would you consider an appropriate sum, bearing in mind the difference between winter and summer bills?

8  Fuel in the home.
(a) Give six safety precautions which must be considered when using gas cookers.
(b) Give clear directions for dealing with a suspected gas leak.
(c) What points should be considered when lighting (i) a kitchen;
(ii) the hall and landing? Give examples.
(d) Electricity is measured in 'watts' but the electricity bill will state the number of 'units' used. What is a 'unit' of electricity?
(e) Give two faults which would cause a fuse to blow. (SEREB)

9   (a) Electricity can be dangerous when improperly used. List five important points to remember for its safe use.
(b) (i) What colour is the earth wire in an electric flex? (ii) Why is it necessary to have electrical appliances earthed? (MREB)

10  What causes hardness in water and what is the difference between temporary and permanent hardness? Describe fully how modern washing powders and water softening equipment overcome the disadvantage of a hard water supply. (O & C)

11  (a) Draw an outline of the British Isles. Using a geological map, mark those areas likely to have a hard water supply.
(b) Find out the approximate cost of installing a water-softening system in your house.

12  (a) What is a mixer tap? Give reasons why you consider it useful in (i) a kitchen; (ii) a bathroom.
(b) (i) Draw a diagram of the 'U' bend pipe under a sink and explain its purpose. (ii) How can the 'U' bend be kept clean? (MREB)

13  Find out the source of your local water supply. Is fluoride added to your drinking water?

There has been much discussion about the advisability of adding fluoride to water supplies. Make a study of the factors for and against it, look for information and comments in the press, on television and radio, and from toothpaste manufacturers. Who actually makes the decision as to whether or not to add fluoride?

14  Make a study of the effect of pollution on the environment, on the air, the soil, and on river and sea water. Look for articles in the press, and on TV and radio. Find out what steps your own water authority takes to detect and prevent pollution.

15  Imagine you have a blocked drain in a kitchen sink. State:
(a) what action you would take
(b) how you would prevent a recurrence.

16  Describe the ways in which all types of household waste are removed from the house.

What action would you take if the dustmen had not been to empty the dustbins for several weeks? (O)

17  Find out the price of buying and installing a waste disposal unit. What priority would you give to buying one, as compared to other household equipment?

18  Draw a diagram to show the exterior walls of your home. Mark on it the position of the different pipes and drains and label them. Look at the exterior of a very new house and note which drainage pipes are visible.

19　Design a poster which could be used to encourage people to keep their dustbins clean and hygienic.

20　(a) How would you actually clean and disinfect a dustbin?
(b) How would you dispose of the following:

(i)　ashes from a coal fire
(ii)　left-over scraps of food
(iii) an empty cat-food tin
(iv) potato peelings
(v)　newspapers and magazines?

21　See if you can arrange a visit to your local refuse disposal plant. Does your local authority have any plans for improving its present system? What do they salvage at present from the waste they collect?

22　(a) Describe two methods by which electric heaters transfer heat in a room.
(b) Before attaching a plug to a new electric fire, by which colour would you recognize each of the following wires?
(i) Live wire; (ii) Earth wire; (iii) Neutral wire
(c) What is the function of each of these wires?
(d) What is the purpose of a fuse cartridge in a plug?
(e) List four safety precautions which should be taken before using electrical appliances in the home. Give reasons for your answers.
(SCE)

---

**Books for further reading**

*Science for Housecraft* **John Robinson** Edward Arnold
*Science in the Home* **Lilian Gawthorpe** Hulton Educational
*Hygiene in the Home* **Elisabeth Norton** Mills and Boon
*Science and your Home* **J. Gostelow** Blond Educational
*At Home with Science* **O. F. G. Kilgour** Heinemann Educational

Leaflets from Electricity Boards
*'Electricity and You'* series, including:
*Easy Ways to Pay*
*Guide to Running Costs*
*How to Read your Meter*
*Plugs and Fuses*
*Warmth without Waste*

# Chapter 3
# Heating the home

# Fires and heaters

Heat transferred from any fire or heater reaches the people in the room either by <u>radiation</u> or <u>convection</u>.

### Radiated heat

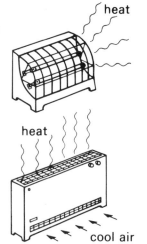

This warms only the solid objects or people it shines on. It does not warm the air between them, nor does it warm the backs of the people or objects it shines on. The sun warms the earth by radiant heat, and a bar electric fire warms by radiant heat.

### Convected heat

This works on the principle of warm air currents rising from the heater and being replaced by cooler air. Currents of air circulate around the room, gradually warming both the air and the people in the room.

We can keep ourselves and our homes warm either by individual fires and heaters, or by central heating. We shall look at central heating systems later in the chapter; we shall now look at the many types of fires and heaters that are available, using solid fuel, gas, electricity or oil.

### Solid-fuel fires

#### *Open coal fires*
Advantages
1   A coal fire has a cheerful, attractive appearance.
2   It can have a back boiler to supply hot water.
3   It helps to ventilate the room. A coal fire needs air to burn, so it is constantly drawing air into the room to replace the air it uses.

Disadvantages
1   A lot of heat goes up the chimney and is wasted.
2   A coal fire causes dust, ashes and soot in the home.
3   A lot of work is involved in cleaning and laying the fire, in stoking it, and in having the chimney swept.
4   As it warms by radiation, only people directly facing the fire will be warm. Their backs may feel cold and people away from the fire may feel cold.
5   It causes a draught in the room as it draws in the air it needs to burn.
6   When the fire is not lit there will be no hot water unless an electric immersion heater is fitted in the hot water tank.
7   Smoke from coal fires causes pollution of the air. This is a health hazard and also causes damage to the stonework of buildings.

### *Enclosed solid-fuel fires or room heaters*
The glow of the fire shows through glass doors. These fires use Solid Smokeless Fuel. This fuel is made from coal which has been treated so that it does not produce smoke.

#### Advantages
1   These fires are quite economical to run as they can be easily controlled.
2   They do not waste as much heat up the chimney as an open fire does.
3   They can heat the hot water and several radiators.
4   The surface of the heater gets hot and sets up convection currents which warm the whole room.

#### Disadvantages
1   The fires are not very attractive to look at.
2   The fire has to be stoked and the ashes cleaned out.
3   The fuel has to be ordered, stored and carried in.

## Smokeless zones

Many areas are now <u>smoke controlled</u>, which means that no houses or factories in the area may burn coal or any fuel which produces smoke. This was enforced by the Clean Air Act of 1956 to try to eliminate the problem of <u>smog</u>. Smog was produced by the mixture of heavy fog with smoke from hundreds of chimneys which could not escape up into the air through the fog. This smog was extremely unhealthy and caused the deaths of many people from bronchitis and other diseases of the lungs.

## Gas fires

Modern gas fires use both radiant and convected heat to warm the room. They have to be fitted into either an existing fireplace with a chimney, or an external wall with a flue door, to ensure adequate ventilation.

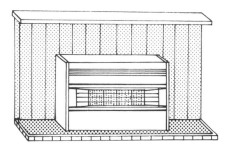

#### Advantages
1   They are simple to use and control, and usually light automatically.
2   They warm the room quickly.
3   Some can heat the hot water if fitted in a fireplace where there is an existing back boiler.
4   Some models can run a central heating system.
5   Their appearance is attractive.

Disadvantages
1  About 25% of the heat produced is lost up the chimney or flue.
2  They must be used in a well-ventilated room to avoid dry air and the build-up of dangerous fumes.
3  They should be serviced every two or three years.

### Mobile gas heaters

These run from bottled gas, e.g. Calor gas. They are not very attractive to look at, but they give off a lot of heat. They are on castors, so they can be moved to wherever you want them. Anyone living temporarily in a house without a good heating system would find them ideal, as when you move house you can take them with you. The bottles of gas are bought in advance, so you avoid unexpectedly high fuel bills.

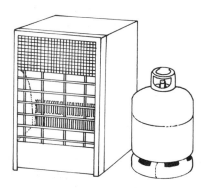

## Electric fires

There are many different kinds of electric fires and heaters available, including fan heaters, radiant fires, convector heaters, and oil-filled portable radiators which are electrically heated. (Night storage heaters also use electricity. These are discussed in the section on central heating. See page 48.)

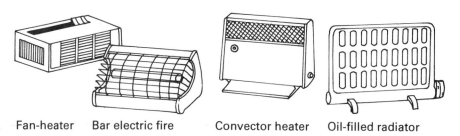

Fan-heater    Bar electric fire        Convector heater    Oil-filled radiator

Advantages
1  Electric fires are very clean and easy to use.
2  They are very efficient, as no heat is wasted up the chimney.
3  Most heaters can be carried to where they are required.
4  They are useful for heating a small area quickly.

Disadvantages
1  They are expensive to run for a long time or for a large area.
2  They do not heat the water.

**Oil heaters**

These may be either the convector type, similar to electric convector heaters, or the radiant type. The fuel they use is paraffin.

 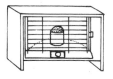

Convector oil heater     Radiant oil heater

Advantages
1 They are the cheapest form of heating to buy and to run.
2 You can carry the heaters to wherever you need the heat.
3 Fuel must be bought before it is used, so you avoid unexpected bills.

Disadvantages
1 They are not very attractive to look at.
2 Some heaters give off an unpleasant smell.
3 They need to be refilled fairly often.
4 They produce a lot of moisture as they burn, and so can encourage dampness and condensation.
5 They can be very dangerous and cause many fires; sometimes the heater is knocked over when alight, or a draught blowing on the heater causes the flame to set fire to material such as curtains.

The Consumer Protection Act of 1961 was passed in an attempt to prevent these fires. It lays down safety standards for all gas, electric and oil heaters now sold. When you go to buy an oil heater you should only buy one marked with the British Standards Institution Kitemark. It will only have this mark if it is safe and:
a has a reliable guard.
b cannot be knocked over easily.
c the flame will go out immediately if it should be knocked over.

---

Questions

1 **What four fuels are used for heating?**
2 **What is meant by radiant heat?**
3 **Describe, with a diagram, how convected heat warms the whole room.**
4 **Why do some people like a coal fire better than any other kind of heating, yet others dislike coal fires?**
5 **What are the advantages of an enclosed solid-fuel fire as compared with an open coal fire?**
6 **Why was the Clean Air Act of 1956 passed?**
7 **What are the points for and against heating a room with a gas fire?**
8 **What kind of gas heater would suit a couple living temporarily in a flat without a good heating system?**
9 **Describe and draw two kinds of electric heater. Say where each would be useful.**
10 **Why should you choose an oil heater with the B.S.I. Kitemark?**

# Central heating

Central heating is a system where heat from just one central source is carried around the whole house.

The systems most commonly used are:

a   A series of radiators around the house containing hot water. The water may be heated by solid fuel, gas or oil.
b   A system which blows warm air into the rooms.
c   Night storage heaters and under-floor heating using off-peak electricity. Night storage heaters are not exactly central heating, but we can look at them here.

## New houses

Nearly all new houses have a central heating system built into them. When choosing a new house you should try to find out whether the system installed will suit your needs.

## Installing heating

If you decide to install central heating in an existing house it will be expensive, but it adds to the comfort and value of the house. Before you decide on the type to install you should get as much information as you can to compare the different kinds on the market. There is always plenty of advice available from gas and electricity board showrooms and from suppliers of solid fuel and oil.

You should carefully consider all the following general points before making your final decision:

1   How much will the system cost to buy and install?
2   What will the approximate running costs be each week?
3   How often should it be serviced?
4   Is it easy to work?
5   Will it cause much dirt in the house?
6   Does the system provide hot water or will a separate water heating system be required?
7   Is it easy to control the heat for economical running?
8   Will it produce enough heat for the whole house, even in the coldest weather?

## Small bore central heating system

This is a system of radiators filled with hot water. The water may be heated by various means:
a gas, oil or solid-fuel boiler
a gas or solid-fuel fire.

The water is forced through the small pipes to the radiators by means of a small electric pump.

All of these systems provide domestic hot water (for baths, washing and laundry) by the indirect system. This water never mixes with the water in the radiators (see page 51).

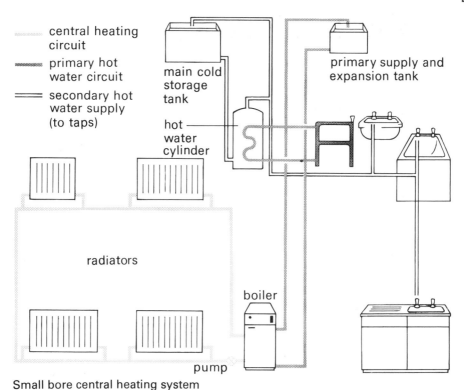

central heating circuit

primary hot water circuit

secondary hot water supply (to taps)

main cold storage tank

hot water cylinder

primary supply and expansion tank

radiators

boiler

pump

Small bore central heating system

### Thermostats

Most systems can be fitted with thermostatic control. The thermostat is fixed to the wall of the room and set to the required temperature, for example, 20°C. When the room reaches this temperature the pump switches off. When the temperature falls below 20°C it switches back on. This helps keep running costs down.

### Time clocks

These are often used with central heating systems. They enable the heating to switch itself on and off automatically at the time you set the clock. This means, for example, that if you came home from work at 6 p.m. you could set the clock to switch on at 4.30 p.m. so that the house would be warm for your return.

**The warm air system**

The air is warmed in a gas heating unit and then blown by an electric fan through metal ducts around the house. The hot air enters each room through grilles in the wall or floor.

As the warm air is carried around the house in large metal ducts, it is not suitable for installing into existing houses but is fitted while a house is being built.

This system can also be fitted with a thermostat and time clock.

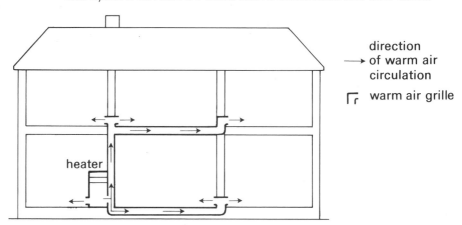

⟶ direction of warm air circulation

⌐ᵣ warm air grille

heater

**Central heating systems run by electricity**

*Night storage heaters*

These heaters are filled with firebricks with an electric element running through them. The electric current heats up the bricks during the night when electricity is cheaper, and slowly gives out the heat during the next day. A separate heater is installed in every room where one is required.

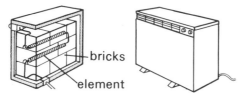

bricks

element

Advantages
1 They are fairly cheap to buy and install.
2 As they use 'off-peak' electricity, which costs less than electricity used during the day, they are not too expensive to run.
3 They keep the room comfortably warm all day, cooling off slowly in the evening.
4 They are clean, easy and quiet to use.

Disadvantages
1 They are rather large and extremely heavy.
2 The heat cannot be quickly controlled.
3 The heat given off during the day would be wasted if there was no one at home during the day.
4 They do not supply hot water.

*Under-floor heating, overhead ceiling heating*

An electric element is embedded either into the concrete floor or into the ceiling panels when the house is being built. This system also normally uses off-peak electricity.

## White meter

If a white meter is installed, then all electricity used at night is charged at the cheaper 'off-peak' rate. The hot water cylinder can be fully heated during the night at this cheaper rate and if well insulated will keep hot for use during the following day. This system is most useful for the family who are at home all day.

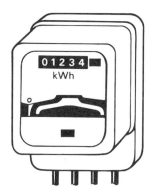

---

Questions

1　**What is the difference between central heating and a fire?**
2　**What are the advantages of central heating?**
3　**Describe the six most important points to consider when installing central heating.**
4　**You have decided to install a small bore central heating system in your house. What method would you choose for heating the water which circulates in the system? List all the advantages of the method you have chosen.**
5　**Describe how a thermostat works and the advantages of having one.**
6　**Why are time-clocks often fitted to heating systems? Give an example of when one would be useful.**
7　**Name three central heating systems which have to be installed while the house is being built.**
8　**You are living in a house built several years ago which at present is heated by open coal fires. Describe one type of central heating which you could install, giving the reasons why the system is suitable.**
9　**An elderly retired couple wish to install a central heating system. What kind would you advise them to choose and what would be its advantages for them?**
10　**Name a central heating system which supplies hot water for domestic use while it warms the house.**
11　**What is 'off-peak' electricity?**
12　**What is a white meter?**

# The domestic hot water supply

A constant supply of hot water is a great advantage to any household. There are many different methods of heating the water, using solid fuel, gas, electricity or oil. Some methods are combined with the heating of the house, while others work independently of it.

When you move into a house there is usually a hot water system installed. If not, you should make careful enquiries to find the system best suited to your particular needs. You should consider these points:

1  The cost of buying the equipment and having it installed.
2  The probable running costs.
3  Suitability for the size and type of family, e.g. how much hot water is required? how often is the family in or out all day?
4  Is the system easy to use?
5  How long does the water take to heat?

## The direct hot water system

In older houses hot water may be provided by a solid-fuel boiler in the kitchen or an open coal fire in the living-room. The water is heated in a small back boiler behind the fire. It rises to and is stored in the cylinder. From there it goes directly to the hot taps.

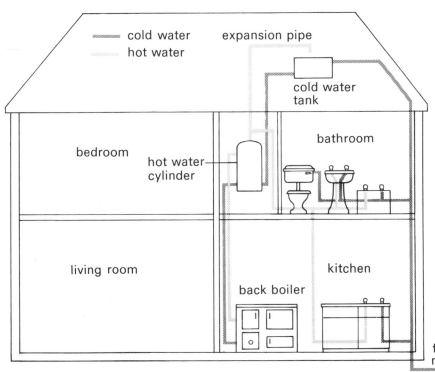

cold water
hot water
expansion pipe
cold water tank
bathroom
bedroom
hot water cylinder
living room
kitchen
back boiler
from mains

**The indirect hot water system**

All central heating systems which provide hot water use the <u>indirect</u> method of water heating. Look again at the central heating diagram on page 47. In this system, the boiler heats water which flows through a coiled pipe inside the hot water tank and back to the boiler. The water in the cylinder is heated by contact with these coiled hot pipes, and is then used to supply the taps. The water in the coiled pipe never changes but passes continually around the system. Being in a closed circuit it never mixes with the hot water supply to the taps.

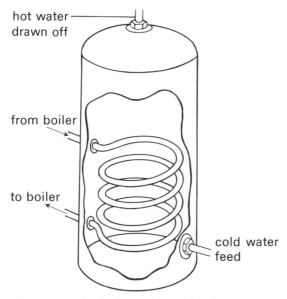

Hot water cylinder heated by coiled pipe

The advantages of the indirect system are:
1 It makes sure that the water inside the radiators, which may become rather rusty, never comes through the taps for household use.
2 It prevents the constant 'furring' of the pipes and boiler, as the same specially softened water passes continually through the boiler. This is particularly important in hard water areas where the whole system might otherwise fur up.

*Hot water only*

If hot water only is required, and not the central heating, the pump which circulates the water around the radiators can just be switched off.

**Heating water by electricity**

This has several advantages:
1 It is very efficient and wastes little heat, as the element is completely immersed in the water. All the heat goes into the water and none is wasted through flues or chimneys.
2 It is clean, easy to use, and easy to control.

<u>But</u> it can be expensive to use electricity to supply constant, large quantities of hot water.

### Different types of electric water heater

1 *Immersion heaters* have an element fitted into the tank like an electric kettle. A twin-immersion heater is very economical to use. This type has two elements, one short and one long. The shorter one heats the top of the tank only and provides plenty of water for daily use. The longer element need only be switched on when large quantities are required for baths and doing the washing.

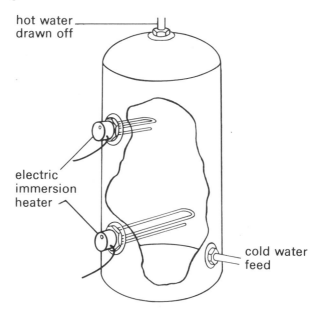

hot water drawn off

electric immersion heater

cold water feed

2 *Storage water heaters* can be fitted near the sink or wash basin, providing smaller or larger quantities of hot water according to their size. These are useful in older houses which do not have a hot water system.

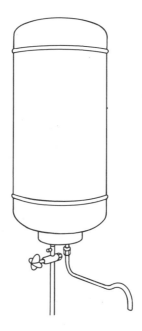

## Heating water by gas

Gas water heaters are mainly of the <u>instantaneous</u> type. They supply endless hot water to one or several taps. When the tap is turned on the cold water passes through a series of narrow pipes which are heated by gas jets. There is no hot water cylinder for storing water with this system as the water is heated instantly and only when required.

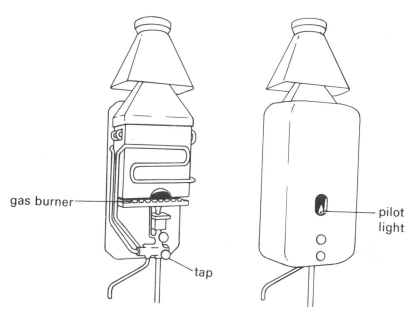

*Gas fires* may have a boiler fitted behind them, so that they heat the water as well as the room. These are often installed when a coal fire with a back boiler is being replaced by a gas fire.

*Gas storage water heaters* are also available. The water is heated by a circulator and stored in the hot water cylinder until required. Some gas central heating systems also provide hot water (see page 46).

---

Questions

1 **How do central heating systems provide hot water?**
2 **What are the points for and against heating water by electricity?**
3 **Why is a twin-immersion heater quite an economical method of water heating for a family?**
4 **You have moved to a flat which has cold water only. What kind of water heater could be installed to give a plentiful supply of hot water to the kitchen sink?**
5 **Describe, with the help of a diagram, how an instantaneous gas water heater works.**

# Insulation

Fuel bills can be very high however you heat your home, so you do not want to waste heat. Good insulation will cut down the amount of heat loss from the house.

Heat loss can be prevented in the following ways:

1 **Insulate your loft**

Heat from the house will rise upwards and escape through the roof. A layer of glass fibre or 'loose-fill' insulating material, 75mm (3") thick will prevent some of this loss. The insulation is easy to lay and the cost of it should be recovered by money saved on fuel after two or three years. Do not insulate <u>below</u> the cold water tank if it is in the loft, as some warmth from the house is needed to prevent the water tank from freezing in winter.

2 **Draughts**

Draughts waste heat and make you feel uncomfortable. They can be prevented by fitting plastic, foam or metal excluder strips around doors and windows.

3 **Cavity walls**

These can be filled with special insulating material to cut down heat loss through the walls. You must choose an approved contractor (covered by an Agrément Certificate) to do the work for you. He will make sure that the walls are suitable for treatment and will guarantee a good job. The work takes about a day and is carried out from the outside by drilling the outer wall, so no mess is caused inside the house.

## 4  Double glazing

This consists of two panes of glass with a sealed air space between them. It cuts down heat loss through windows and reduces noise and condensation. It makes the room feel more comfortable as the area near the window does not feel cold.

Double glazing is very expensive, and it would take many years to recover the cost in money saved in fuel. It may however be worth double-glazing the windows in the main living-room. Thick, lined curtains are a much less expensive but very effective way of reducing heat loss.

## 5  Floors and chimneys

Thick carpets and underlays save heat. Unused fireplaces can be blocked but should be partly ventilated to prevent condensation in the chimney.

## 6  The hot water tank

Much of the cost of water heating can be saved by lagging the tank with a jacket at least 75mm (3″) thick. This is easy to fit and cheap – it could pay for itself in two or three months. Most modern houses are supplied with lagged tanks. It is wasteful to leave the tank unlagged just to provide an airing cupboard. Some tanks are available with insulation already fitted.

Hot water pipes should be lagged, and cold pipes also need insulating to prevent freezing in winter.

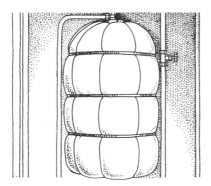

---

## Questions

1  **Why should you insulate your home as well as possible?**
2  **Describe how and why you would insulate your loft.**
3  **How could you get rid of draughts?**
4  **How does cavity-wall insulation work?**
5  **How would you choose a firm to insulate the cavity walls in your home?**
6  **Double glazing is very expensive. Suggest another way of reducing the heat loss through windows.**
7  **What are the advantages of double glazing?**
8  **Why should a hot water tank be well lagged?**
9  **What is the best way to do this?**

# Ventilation

Ventilation means exchanging the stale air in a room for fresh air. If the air in a room remained still and unchanged the room would soon feel stuffy and uncomfortable, and it would make you feel tired.

When you ventilate a room, you remove the stale air which contains uncomfortable amounts of moisture, smoke, steam, warmth and carbon dioxide, and replace it with fresh air.

Ventilation is helped by the natural upward movement of currents of warm air which are replaced by cooler air. It is important to try to introduce fresh air into a room without causing draughts.

There are several different methods of ventilating a room:

## 1 A coal fire

Hot air rises up the chimney and cool air is drawn from the room to replace it. Although this method provides good ventilation, it can often feel very draughty to the people in the room.

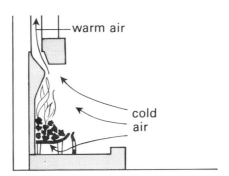

## 2 Doors and windows

Open doors and windows provide ventilation. Where a small window can be left open at the top, fresh air can be brought into the room without causing a draught.

## 3 Air bricks

These may be set high in the outside wall of a room which does not have ventilation through a fireplace, for example, in a bedroom, bathroom or W.C. They are found mainly in older houses.

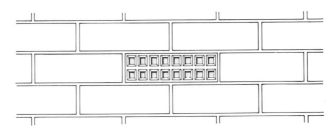

### 4 Extractor fan

This can be set in the window. It works electrically and draws stale air and cooking smells out of the kitchen. It is fairly expensive to install and is rather noisy in use.

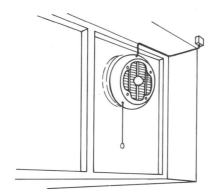

### 5 A Cooper's disc

This is inserted in a window and may be turned to the open or the closed position.

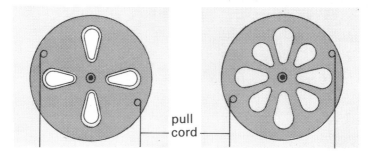

pull
cord

### 6 Air conditioning

This is a complete system which controls both the temperature and the humidity (moisture content) of the air being circulated around a building. Air-conditioning systems are not built into houses in this country but are widely used in modern office blocks, factories and large stores.

---

Questions

1 **Why is it necessary to ventilate rooms?**
2 **How does a coal fire ventilate a room?**
3 **What is the disadvantage of ventilating a room by means of a coal fire?**
4 **Describe a method of ventilation which would be suitable for:**
a **a living-room**
b **a bathroom**
c **a kitchen**
d **a department store.**

# Lighting

Good lighting in the home is important. It helps to prevent eye-strain and accidents, and to create a cheerful, homely atmosphere.

The best, most even kind of light is natural sunlight. The amount of sunlight a room receives will depend on the position and size of the windows.

Artificial light is provided by electricity. It is easy to use and control, and it is inexpensive.

Different kinds of lighting are suitable for different areas of the house. A kitchen needs to be well lit, and for this fluorescent strip lighting is particularly suitable. It is economical to run and provides good light with no shadows. A 100 or 150 watt bulb is suitable for the centre light in a room. 60 watt bulbs can be used for table lamps, spotlights, and floor standing lamps, to provide extra light for close work such as reading or sewing.

## Light fittings

Light fittings are used to avoid the harsh glare of the light bulb and to produce different effects.

1  *Direct lighting.* The bulb is covered by a shade which sends all the light downwards. This is most suitable for close work.
2  *Indirect lighting.* The bulb is completely concealed by the shade and the light is reflected up to the ceiling and on to the walls. This is most suitable for wall lights and halls.
3  *General lighting.* The bulb is enclosed in a translucent fitting, and light is sent out in all directions. This is suitable for all rooms.

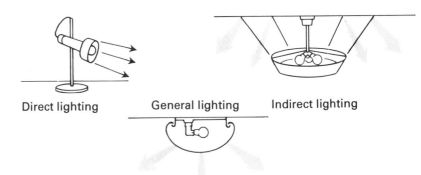

Direct lighting  General lighting  Indirect lighting

A pendant light in the centre of the room gives more light than wall lights of the same wattage. Table lamps and floor-standing lamps can provide extra lighting around the room. Spotlights can be directed on to pictures or ornaments, and a lighting track allows you to move spotlights to highlight different areas of the room. In the dining-room, a 'rise-and-fall' fitment can be used over the table.

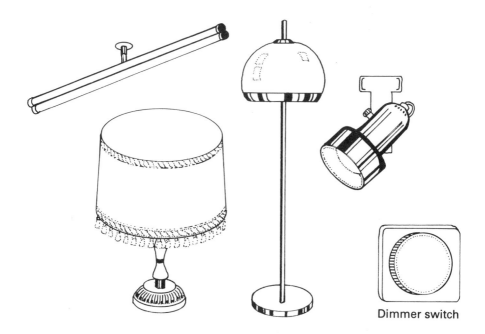

Dimmer switch

**Economy in lighting**

Although lighting costs make up only a small proportion of the electricity bill (most of the cost goes on heating and hot water), some economies can still be made to reduce lighting costs.

1 Lights can be switched off when not in use, but for safety the stairs should always be well lit.
2 Soft general lighting with work areas more brightly lit is better and cheaper than bright lighting for the whole room.
3 Dimmer switches can be used to reduce the amount of lighting required. This is both economical and attractive.
4 Low wattage bulbs, e.g. 40W, 60W, can safely be used in the bedrooms, bathroom and W.C.
5 Coloured shades can be changed for lighter shades which give out more light.
6 Fluorescent lights are cheaper to run.

Questions

1 **How are light fittings used to produce
(a) direct, (b) indirect, and (c) general lighting?
For which areas of the house is each suitable?**
2 **Suggest a plan for producing suitable and attractive lighting for
(a) a living/dining-room, (b) a kitchen, and (c) a hall.
Give reasons for your suggestions.**
3 **Name some safe ways of reducing the cost of lighting.**

# Further work on chapter 3

1   Discuss the advantages and disadvantages of each of the following
    methods of heating a family living-room:
    (a) a night storage heater
    (b) an oil convector heater
    (c) a radiant gas fire.
    State what precautions are necessary where there are children. (O)

2   What is the difference between heating by convection and by
    radiation? Explain, using a diagram to help you, how a convector
    heater warms a room.

3   (a) Name three kinds of central heating.
    (b) Which kind would you choose? Why?
    (c) State two ways of insulating the home against heat loss. (O)

4   You are considering installing central heating into your home, an
    'average' three-bedroom semi-detached house. Find out what
    temperatures are considered suitable for the living-room, bedrooms,
    and bathroom. Collect detailed information on three possible systems
    you could install. Compare:
    (a) the installation costs
    (b) the expected running costs per year and per week.

5   Describe three ways in which the stale air in a room can be replaced
    by fresh air.

6   Do a project on insulation based on your own home. Find out the
    names of some reputable firms in your area who carry out loft
    insulation, double glazing and cavity-wall insulation. Compare their
    costs with Do-It-Yourself methods. Try to collect samples, diagrams,
    illustrations and figures. This can be done individually or in a group
    and a display can be made of your results.

7   Produce a folder on lighting, to include some or all of the following:
    (a) The invention of the electric lamp (bulb).
    (b) How filament lamps and fluorescent lamps work.
    (c) A room plan for a living/dining-room illustrating an attractive
    lighting scheme. Give a guide to the cost of the fitments.

**Books for further reading**

*At Home with Science* **O. F. G. Kilgour** Heinemann Educational
*Hygiene in the Home* **Elisabeth Norton** Mills and Boon
*Science and your Home* **J. Gostelow** Blond Educational
*Science for Housecraft* **John Robinson** Edward Arnold
Booklets from electricity and gas showrooms, and from solid fuel
advisory service (see your telephone directory for address)

# Chapter 4
# **Furniture and furnishings**

# Room planning

Choosing colour schemes and furnishings for a room so that it looks really attractive is much more difficult than it appears. You should spend a lot of time on careful planning before making any final choice, if you want a good effect.

Any mistakes you make, such as choosing the wrong colour carpet, can be so expensive that you will have to live with it for a long time, even though it irritates you every time you look at it.

When you plan and furnish any room you will nearly always have to keep certain items – it is not very often that you can buy everything new. Always take these furnishings into account when you choose colours and patterns for your new scheme.

Planning any room involves: choice of decorations; furniture; carpets; curtains and soft furnishings; and lighting.

## Colour schemes

The most important factor in deciding whether or not a room looks well planned is colour. If you can choose the colours of everything in the room so that they look good together, then you are well on the way to having an attractive room.

Getting colours to match and blend to give the effect you want is not easy and does not often happen by accident. It is very useful if you know a little bit about colour before you start.

The three main colours are red, yellow and blue. By mixing and blending these three you can make up most other colours.

Look carefully at the colour wheel on the back cover and you will see how the other colours are produced as these three gradually blend together.

### Choosing colours which go well together

1   Use the colour wheel to help you choose colours which will go well together, and to avoid a clash.
2   Avoid placing colours from opposite sides of the wheel beside each other, as the contrast between them will tend to be vivid and harsh. Examples of this are orange and blue, or red and green.
3   Colours which are fairly close on the wheel will give a softer, more pleasant contrast, as they blend together naturally.

### Other points about colour

1   Some colours give a warm feeling to a room, for example, red, orange, and yellow. They can brighten up a room which does not get much natural sunlight.
2   Other colours create a cool, restful atmosphere in a room, for example, blue and green. They would be suitable for a room which had plenty of sunlight.
3   *Neutrals* such as white, cream, grey or black are not really colours. They will link your colour scheme together.
4   Several different shades of the same colour can be used together. A shade is a lighter or darker version of the same colour (made by adding some white or black to the basic colour).

### Choosing your colour scheme

1 The main colour should be chosen first – choose one you really like and will not tire of too quickly, and which is either warm or cool to suit the room.

2 A neutral colour should be chosen next to link the scheme together, for example, white, cream or grey.

3 A contrasting colour in small amounts gives interest. This may come from opposite your main colour on the wheel for a vivid, lively contrast, or from nearer to the main colour on the wheel for a softer, less startling, contrast. This colour could be used for lamp shades, cushions or rugs.

4 Plan around any furnishings or carpet you have to keep and always fit them into any new scheme.

5 The most expensive items are probably the carpet and armchairs. If these are chosen in a neutral shade you will be able to change your colour scheme quite simply when you feel like it, by changing the colours used for smaller items, like cushions, lamps or an alcove wall.

#### Texture

Texture can be brought into your scheme to make surfaces look more interesting. Texture means the way a material or surface feels when you touch it. A very smooth material like cotton has no texture but a material with a raised pile or weave, such as rough tweed, velvet, or a long-pile carpet has texture. It will look and feel more interesting than a smooth, flat material.

#### Pattern

Some pattern in a room provides interest and is useful for hiding marks and general wear and tear. Too much pattern in any room will make it look cluttered and busy. As a general rule, never have more than one large pattern in a room. If, for example, you choose a highly patterned carpet to hide the usual marks of family wear, you should avoid having a vividly patterned wallpaper or curtains as well. A very small, neat, overall pattern could be used as well, though, and could look very attractive.

Matching wallpaper and material for curtains, cushion covers or bedspreads can be bought in some very attractive designs, although they can be rather expensive.

---

### Questions

1 **What effect do colours from opposite each other on the wheel give when placed together?**

2 **Name three pairs of colours which show this rather harsh contrast.**

3 **What effect do colours near each other on the wheel give when placed together?**

4 **Suggest three pairs of colours which you think would give a pleasing contrast in a room.**

5 **List the five most important rules to remember when planning a colour scheme.**

6 **Plan a colour scheme for a bedroom for yourself, following the rules given above. Say what colours you would use for a carpet, the walls, a bedspread, the curtains and the lampshades. Where would you bring in some pattern and texture?**

7 **Suggest a scheme suitable for a family living-room.**

# Choosing furniture

Furniture should be very carefully chosen as it is expensive and receives a lot of hard wear. As the cost is so high, it may suit you to buy new furniture on hire-purchase (see page 130). If a piece of furniture is well made it will stay in good condition long after it has been paid for, but if it is of poor quality it will soon look shabby.

Good second-hand furniture from sales or friends may be a better buy than badly-made new items. It can be improved with new paint and covers and can be replaced later when you can afford it.

## Points to consider before buying any furniture

1   Which pieces do you really need?
2   Is it solidly made?
3   Will it be easily marked?
4   How should you clean or polish it?
5   Will it match the rest of your furniture?
6   What will it look like after a couple of years of family use?
7   How long must you wait for delivery?
8   What can you afford to pay, in cash or by hire-purchase?
9   Can you buy the same item more cheaply at a furniture discount warehouse?
10   Does it have a Design Centre label?

Look for the Design Centre label attached to furniture. It shows that it has been selected by the Council of Industrial Design as being a well-designed article. That is, it is of good quality, well made for its purpose and attractive in appearance.

## Choosing particular pieces of furniture

### Tables
1   The table should be large enough for all the family. Some can have an extra leaf added, and others fold down when not in use.
2   It should be steady and should not wobble. Check this carefully with a 'drop-leaf' folding table.
3   The finish is important. It should be fairly resistant to scratches and heat. Most tables need protection against hot plates by table mats.
4   Tables with Formica or Melamine tops are popular for daily use as they are resistant to heat and scratches and they can be washed.

### Chairs
1   Dining chairs should be firm and support the back comfortably.
2   Easily cleaned chairs are needed when there are children who may spill food.
3   The chairs should be the right height for the table with which they are used.

### Sideboard
1   This can be useful for storing cutlery, table cloths and other items.
2   It should have plenty of drawer and cupboard space.
3   If it is a suitable height it can be used for serving meals.

### Armchairs and settees

1 They should be comfortable. A high back gives more support to the head than a low back.
2 The frame and cushions should be firmly made but not too heavy.
3 The cover should be firmly woven to stand up to daily use.
4 The colour should be practical so that it will not show every mark.
5 A three-piece suite is not always the best choice. Individual chairs may suit the family better.
6 A settee which converts to a bed may be useful for visitors.

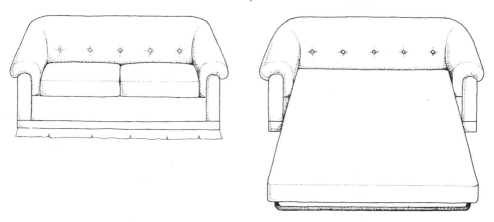

7 Many armchairs and settees have foam-filled cushions and padding. Sometimes they are easily inflammable, that is, they catch fire easily. If this should happen, the fumes from the foam can be very dangerous. All new furniture with this fire risk is sold now with a warning label attached to it.

### Beds

1   As you spend about one-third of your life in bed, you should buy the best you can afford. The standard widths are 150 cms for a double bed, 100 cms for a single. The length is 200 cms.

2   Bunk beds save a lot of space in a smaller home, but they are often only 75 cms wide.

3   Modern beds are divans, consisting of a base which should be really firm, and a mattress. You may prefer either a firm or a soft mattress. Always lie down on the mattress to test it before you buy.

4   Mattresses may be filled with foam or springs. A good foam mattress is firm and comfortable, does not need turning and does not make dust.

5   Spring mattresses vary in quality. The best are usually the most expensive but they will stay comfortable for much longer. They contain individually pocketed springs. There may be up to 2000 inside a double mattress.

6   Headboards are sold separately from the divan bed. They should be firm enough to take the weight of someone leaning against them. They can be very attractive and may be made of wood, Dralon velvet, brass or cane.

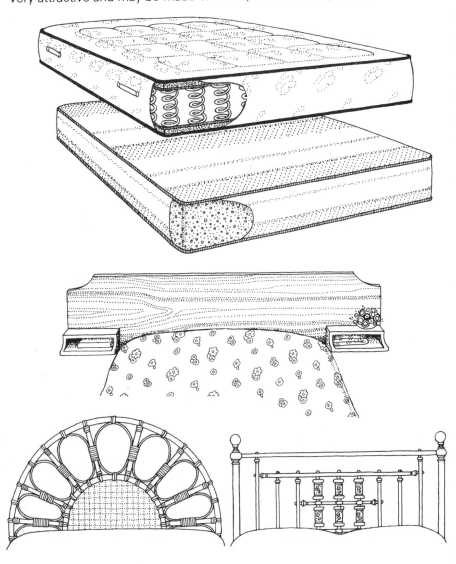

### Wardrobes

1 Wardrobes should be deep enough for a coat hanger and long enough for a long dress. Shelves inside may be useful.
2 Fitted wardrobes, often combined with a dressing-table and chest of drawers, are popular. They can be fixed to the wall, reaching to the ceiling, so they provide plenty of storage space and avoid dust collecting on top.

### Chest of drawers

1 The drawers should be firmly made, preferably with corners 'dove-tailed' rather than glued.

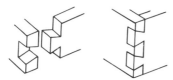

2 They should fit well, run smoothly, and be smoothly finished inside.
3 Handles should be comfortable and easy to hold.

### Dressing-table

1 There should be a good mirror and a shallow drawer for cosmetics.
2 The surface should not be too easily marked by spilt perfume or make-up.
3 Make sure there is enough space below for your knees, so that you can sit comfortably.

---

### Questions

1 **How can a young couple make their money go as far as possible when they are buying furniture?**
2 **What do you think are the four most important points to consider when choosing any furniture, and why?**
3 **What furniture do you think is necessary for (a) a living-room with a dining area at one end, and (b) a bedroom?**
4 **What must you look out for when choosing (a) a table and chairs, (b) armchairs, (c) a bed, (d) a wardrobe, (e) a chest of drawers, and (f) a dressing-table?**
5 **Draw the Design Centre label and explain what it means.**

# Materials used to make furniture

**Wood**

### Hardwood

For example, teak, mahogany, oak. These trees take a long time to grow so their wood is expensive, but firm and hard-wearing. It is used to make good, solid furniture or to make veneers, and is attractive to look at.

Veneers are extremely thin layers of attractive, good quality wood stuck on to the front of furniture made from cheaper, softer wood to improve its appearance.

### Softwood

For example, pine and spruce. It grows more quickly and so is less hard-wearing, but cheaper. It is used to make the base of veneered furniture and to make unpainted whitewood furniture.

Solid pine furniture is popular and attractive but gets marked more easily than a solid hardwood such as teak.

### Chipboard

This is made by treating wood with resins. It is used to make a lot of modern, inexpensive furniture. The chipboard is finished with either:

a   a veneer of better quality wood.

b   a plastic such as Formica or Melamine, often with a white or wood-grain finish. This is used in kitchen furniture and 'unit' furniture for bedrooms and living-rooms. It is fairly cheap, it can be cleaned by washing, and it resists heat and scratches.

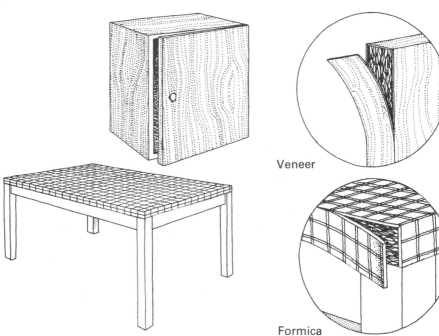

Veneer

Formica

### Other materials

*Metal* e.g. chrome – for arms and legs of tables and chairs.

*Plastic* can be moulded to make lightweight, easily cleaned chairs and tables.

*Leather* is expensive, attractive and hard-wearing. Imitation leather or P.V.C. is much cheaper, fairly hard-wearing and easy to clean.

*Dralon* is used for armchairs and settees. It has a soft, velvety appearance, but is tough and easily shampooed.

### How to look after wood surfaces

Wood in its natural state is easily marked, so it has to have a 'finish' or seal. This may be one of the following:

| *Finish on the wood* | *How to clean and care for it* |
|---|---|
| *Cellulose* Used on tables, chairs, school desks. Not easily marked. | Remove marks with damp cloth, dry. Polish occasionally. Protect from heat. |
| *Teak veneer* or *solid teak* Used for bedroom/dining-room furniture. | Do not polish. Rub with teak oil about three times a year. |
| *French polish* Used on older, expensive furniture. Gives a high gloss. Easily marked by heat and scratches. | Remove marks with warm, damp cloth. Dry well. Polish with furniture cream. Protect from heat. |
| *Wax* The original polish for wood. Used on old oak furniture and pine. | Use wax polish sparingly. Rub well to bring out shine. |
| *Paint* Mainly used for kitchen and nursery furniture. | Wash with warm soapy water. Rinse and dry well. |
| *Plastic laminates* e.g. Formica. Widely used for cheaper furniture and for kitchens. | Can be washed and dried frequently without harm. Resists heat and scratches. |

Questions
1 **Name three hardwoods. Why are they expensive?**
2 **How are hardwoods used in furniture?**
3 **What is a veneer?**
4 **What kind of furniture is often made from softwood?**
5 **Name some pieces of furniture often made from chipboard.**
6 **What are the advantages of chipboard furniture?**
7 **How would you care for the following to keep them in good condition?**
a **a Formica-topped bench in the kitchen.**
b **a teak dining-table.**
c **a white painted cupboard in a child's bedroom.**
d **the wooden arms and legs of an easy chair.**

# Carpets

Buying carpets can be very expensive. Always go to a shop where you can trust the assistant to give you good advice. Most carpets look attractive when they are new, but you need other information if you want to know how they will look after a few years' use.

### Grades of carpet

Always look for the labels attached to carpets, which tell you how hard-wearing you can expect the carpets to be. These are the grades you will find:

*Light domestic* – for bedrooms only, where there is very little wear.

*Medium domestic* – where there is only a little more wear, e.g. in a dining-room which is not in everyday use.

*General domestic* – suitable for anywhere in the house.

*Heavy domestic* – very good for areas receiving a lot of wear, e.g. hall or living-room.

*Luxury domestic* – luxurious and hard-wearing, it can be used anywhere.

### Underlay

A good underlay makes carpets last much longer and feel softer and thicker. It also helps keep heat in the room. It is made from thick felt, or foam rubber with a special backing.

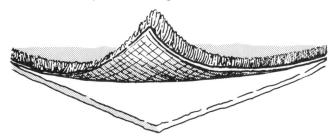

Many cheaper carpets have a built-in foam underlay to make them softer and longer-lasting. A layer of specially thick paper should always be laid between this kind of carpeting and the floor below, or the foam may stick to the floor and tear when you try to lift it.

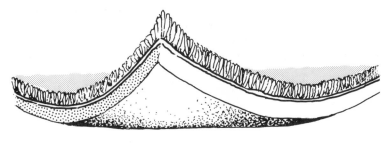

## Points to remember when choosing carpets

### The colour

The colour should tone in with the rest of the furnishings in the room. Dark colours show threads and crumbs, very light colours are easily marked.

### The pattern

A plain carpet will show every mark. A very vivid pattern will not show marks, but you may soon get tired of it. Too many patterns in a room, on the carpet, curtains, walls and cushions, look cluttered and unattractive.

### Fitted carpet, square or tiles?

Fitted carpets are expensive, but are easy to clean and give a spacious, luxurious look to a room.

A carpet square is less expensive. It can easily be moved to a different room or house and can be turned around to help it wear more easily or to hide a stain.

Tiles are easy to lay and fit. Any worn or marked square can be moved to where it will not show.

## Caring for your carpets

### New carpets

Some carpets shed fluff when new. You should leave them to 'settle' for a couple of months and clean them with a sweeper or brush, not a vacuum cleaner. Later, vacuum two or three times a week, and sweep or brush in between.

### Shampoo

Choose a suitable pattern and colour and you will not have to shampoo too often. Nylon and acrylic carpets are easy to shampoo and quick to dry, but attract dirt more than a wool carpet.

Use a foam carpet shampoo. A vacuum cleaner will remove the dirt and shampoo together when the carpet dries. Choose a warm day and do not get the carpet too wet. Let it dry completely before putting the furniture back.

---

Questions

1  **List the five grades of carpet. For which part of the house is each one suitable?**
2  **How can you find out what grade a carpet is when you are in a shop?**
3  **Which grade would you expect to be (a) cheapest, and (b) most expensive?**
4  **How would you expect the carpet to wear if you put (a) a medium domestic in the living-room, (b) a light domestic in the hall, and (c) a general domestic in the dining-room?**
5  **What are the advantages of having a good underlay?**
6  **How must you prepare the floor before laying a foam-backed carpet? Why?**
7  **What must you remember when choosing the pattern and colour of a carpet?**
8  **What are the good and bad points of a carpet square?**

# How carpets are made

The way in which a carpet can be expected to last, without becoming worn and shabby, depends on two main points:

1   The <u>construction</u> of the carpet (the way it is made).
2   The <u>fibre</u> it is made from.

### The construction of carpets

The terms 'Axminster', 'Wilton', 'tufted' and 'corded' apply to the way the carpet is made, not to who makes it, or what it is made from.

#### Axminster and Wilton

These are both <u>woven</u> carpets. The pile and the backing are woven together in a way which produces a firm, well-made carpet.

If an Axminster or Wilton is made of 100% wool, or 80% wool and 20% nylon, the carpet will be top quality, luxurious in appearance and hard-wearing.

But if an Axminster or Wilton is made of a mixture of rayon and wool, then the carpet will be of lower quality, perhaps suitable only for medium domestic use.

The terms Axminster and Wilton, then, do not always mean that a carpet is of the best quality. The quality also depends on the fibre used.

The difference between an Axminster and a Wilton is in the way they are woven. An Axminster can include more colours and pattern than a Wilton, which can only have up to three colours and a simpler pattern, though the carpet may be slightly thicker.

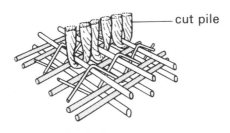

— cut pile

#### Tufted carpets

These have the backing produced first, then the pile stitched into it. A further backing is then added, often of foam rubber, to keep it firm. Tufted carpets are made of various fibres and are fairly inexpensive, but they are not as firm and hard-wearing as good woven carpets.

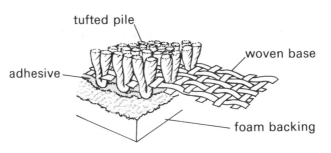

tufted pile

woven base

adhesive

foam backing

*Cord carpets*

These are woven in a similar way to Axminster and Wilton, with a firm, tight loop. They have no pile and are usually very hard-wearing, depending on the fibre used (often hair or sisal). They are not soft to touch, being firm and rather hard, but they provide an attractive, long-lasting fitted carpet at a very reasonable price.

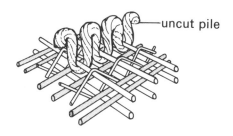
uncut pile

**The fibres used to make carpets**

Carpets are made mainly from wool, nylon, acrylic and rayon. The fibre used is very important in deciding how long the carpet will wear.

1   *Wool* is usually accepted as being the best fibre. Up to 20% nylon is sometimes added for extra strength. It is warm, thick, soft and resilient (it will not flatten in use). It does not get dirty easily but it is expensive.

2   *Acrylic.* Brand names include Acrilan and Courtelle. Acrylic is more like wool than any other man-made fibre, being warm, resilient and soft. It attracts dirt more easily than wool, but is easier to clean and less expensive.

3   *Nylon.* Brand names include Bri-nylon and Enkalon. Strong and hard-wearing, it attracts dirt, but is easy to shampoo and dries quickly. It is suitable for use in a kitchen. It does not feel as soft and warm to touch as wool.

4   *Rayon.* Brand names include Evlan. This is not a resilient fibre so the pile soon flattens. It picks up dirt easily. Its advantage is its low cost, but it does not wear well. It is often mixed with wool or other fibres to make them cheaper.

---

Questions

1   **Name three different methods used to manufacture carpets.**
2   **What are the two main factors which decide how hard-wearing a carpet will be?**
3   **What is the difference between an Axminster and a Wilton?**
4   **Is an Axminster always a best quality carpet? Why is this?**
5   **What are the good and bad points of (a) a tufted carpet, and (b) a cord carpet?**
6   **What are the fibres most often used to make carpets?**
7   **What are (a) the advantages, and (b) the disadvantages of each of these fibres?**

# Curtains

### Choosing the material

1  Look for a colour and pattern which will go with the rest of the furnishings in the room.

2  Ask if the material can be washed, either by hand or machine. If it has to be dry-cleaned, this is much more expensive.

3  Many curtain materials shrink in the wash. You should ask about this before you buy, and allow extra length to let the hem down if necessary after washing.

4  Ask if the material is colour-fast, or whether the colours will run into each other when the curtains are washed. This is especially important when there are several different colours in the material.

### Making the curtains

You can choose whether to have your curtains reaching to the window sill, just below the sill or to the floor.

If you have radiators below the window, never cover them with long curtains or they will not warm the room and the curtains may be spoilt by being so close to the radiator.

Measuring is important to make sure you buy the right amount of material so that the curtains will hang attractively. You must allow at least $1\frac{1}{2}$ times the width of the curtain track if the curtain is to look full enough. If for example the curtain track is 300 cm wide you need 450 cm of material across the top.

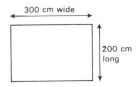

300 cm wide

200 cm long

Curtain material is usually about 120 cm wide so you will need four 'drops' or curtains which will give you 4×120 cm = 480 cm width (or 4 m 80 cm). 25 cm of material has to be added to the length of each 'drop' or curtain, to allow for the hem, the heading, and in case of shrinkage.
So for the window in the diagram above you would have to add 4×25 = 100 cm for the four curtain lengths.

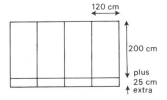

120 cm

200 cm

plus 25 cm extra

The amount of material you would need altogether would therefore be 4×225 cm = 900 cm = 9 metres.

### Lining

It is a good idea to line curtains, because:

1 It stops the curtains fading in the sun.
2 It makes them hang better and look fuller.
3 It helps keep the heat inside the room and the cold air out.

The linings can be sewn into the curtains or they can be detachable to make it easier to wash them.

### Ready-made curtains

These can be bought to fit most windows. This is quite a lot more expensive than making your own, but it does ensure that the curtains are well made and attractive.

### Venetian blinds

These can be used instead of curtains, or as well as curtains to give privacy. When they are open, people in the room can see out but no one can see inside. However, they are expensive to buy, awkward to clean and they look rather bare without curtains as well.

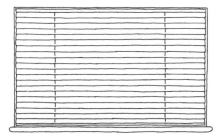

### Roller blinds

These can be bought or made from do-it-yourself kits, in many attractive patterns. They are less expensive than Venetian blinds, though not as long-lasting. They work on a spring and can be 'set' in any position.

Questions

1 **What are the most important points to remember when buying curtain material?**
2 **How much curtain material 120 cm wide would you need for a window (a) 200 cm wide×175 cm deep, (b) 480 cm wide×225 cm deep?**
3 **Why is it a good idea to line your curtains?**
4 **Ready-made curtains are fairly expensive but they have several advantages. List as many as you can think of.**

# Choosing bedding

**Sheets**

Sheets should be big enough for your bed, so that they will stay tucked in properly.

For the standard single bed 100 cm wide, the sheets should be about 175 cm×260 cm.
For the standard double bed 150 cm wide, the sheets should be about 230 cm×260 cm.

### Fitted sheets

You can buy pairs of 'fitted' sheets where the bottom sheet is elasticated, fits tightly around the mattress and cannot come undone. The top sheet is fitted only at the foot of the bed and can be folded back over the blankets. The disadvantage of these fitted sheets is that their position cannot be changed around from top to bottom as a flat sheet can.

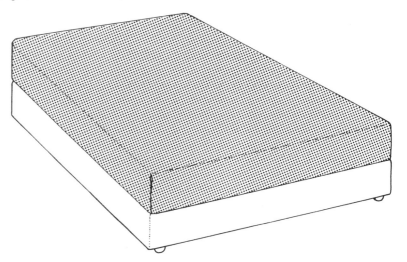

### Materials

The most popular materials for making sheets are cotton, flannelette, polyester and cotton, and nylon.

*Cotton* sheets feel cool and comfortable. Good quality cotton is very hard-wearing. These sheets need ironing, are usually available in plain colours only and are rather expensive.

*Flannelette* or brushed cotton sheets feel soft and warm to the touch when you get into bed. They tend to be less hard-wearing than smooth cotton.

*Polyester and cotton mixture.* These are available in many attractive colours and patterns. They feel quite smooth to the touch and are less expensive than pure cotton. They are easy to wash, quick to dry and need very little ironing.

*Nylon* sheets are quite cheap but many people find them uncomfortable to sleep in as they are not absorbent. They are very easy to wash, quick to dry and need no ironing. They can be smooth or have a warmer, brushed finish.

## Pillowcases

Pillowcases are available to match most sheets and are usually sold in pairs. The normal size is 50 cm × 75 cm.

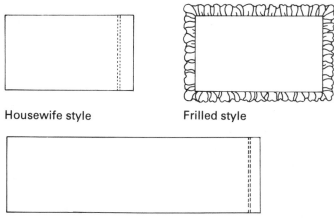

Housewife style        Frilled style

Bolster case for double bed

You should always use an extra pillowslip between the pillow and the pillowcase, to keep the pillow itself really clean.

## Blankets

Blankets can be bought with plain hems, or with the ends bound, in many attractive colours. Cellular woven blankets are warm as they trap pockets of warm air.

Blankets are usually made of:

a  *Wool.* Warm and hard-wearing, these are the best blankets. Check to see if they are machine-washable and moth-proofed.

b  *Acrylic fibre.* These include Acrilan and Courtelle. They are easily washed and dried, moths will not attack them and they are less expensive than wool.

c  *Viscose fibre.* These are the cheapest blankets. They are less warm and do not wash very well as they flatten. Buy better quality if you can. One wool blanket will be warmer and last longer than two poor quality blankets.

## Eiderdowns

Eiderdowns can be as warm as two or three blankets. They can be filled with down or feathers, or if filled with Terylene or other man-made fibres they can be easily washed and dried.

## Bedspreads

Bedspreads make the bed look tidy, and keep the dust off the bedding. They should match the colour scheme of the room. There are many attractive materials to choose from, such as candlewick, cotton or quilted nylon.

### Continental quilts (duvets)

These are lightweight quilts with a special filling, used instead of blankets and other bed-covers.

They are popular as they have many advantages:

1 They are very warm in winter and cool in summer.
2 They make bed-making very quick and easy, as they only need to be shaken and replaced.
3 They do not create dust and fluff.
4 You only need the quilt in its cover over you, cutting out the need for a top sheet, blankets, eiderdown and bedspread.
5 You can buy very attractive matching covers, bottom sheets, valances and pillowcases, in many colours and patterns.
6 As you do not have to buy blankets and other bed-covers, they are not too expensive to buy and they last a very long time.

The quilt can be filled with any of these fillings:

a *Pure down* – very soft, light, warm and expensive. Down is the fine soft underfeathers of ducks or other birds.
b *Feathers and down mixed* – this mixture is most often chosen. Neither down nor feathers can be washed or cleaned.
c *Terylene P3* – a special fibre produced for quilts. It is washable, so it is the most suitable choice of filling for children.

It is important that the quilt is about 45 cm wider than the bed it is for, so that there will be an overlap on both sides.

Continental quilts have a 'tog' rating which indicates how warm you can expect the quilt to be. The tog rating ranges from 7·5 to 10·5 togs. The higher the tog rating, the warmer the quilt. Look for the B.S.I. Kitemark when you go to buy a quilt.

## Pillows

Pillows can be filled with down, feathers, Terylene or foam rubber. The more expensive the pillow, the longer it will usually stay comfortable. You need two pillows for a single bed and four pillows or a bolster and two pillows for a double bed.

## Towels

Towels can be bought in many attractive colours to match the colour scheme in your bathroom. Darker shades have to be washed on their own several times as the colour can run.

Towels vary in size:

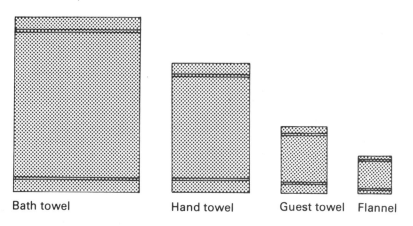

Bath towel      Hand towel      Guest towel    Flannel

Questions

1 **What size should sheets and blankets be to fit (a) a single bed, and (b) a double bed?**
2 **What are the points for and against buying fitted sheets for all your beds?**
3 **Name four materials often used to make sheets. What are the advantages and disadvantages of each one?**
4 **What kind of blankets are usually (a) the warmest, (b) the cheapest, (c) the most easily machine-washed, (d) liable to be attacked by moths, and (e) the most expensive?**
5 **Give as many reasons as you can why many people buy continental quilts rather than blankets and other bed-covers.**
6 **Name a filling suitable for a continental quilt for a 4-year-old child.**
7 **What special care must you take when washing a new set of dark-coloured bath towels?**

# Keeping your home clean

A house which is clean, tidy and well cared for is always a good background for family life. The more efficiently you can plan and carry out your housework, the more time you will have free to enjoy the company of your family and to follow your other interests and hobbies.

The amount of time you spend on housework will depend on:

1  How well organized you are.
2  Whether you and your family are at home, school or work all day.
3  How much you enjoy or dislike housework.
4  How much help you have from labour-saving appliances or from other people.

## Daily routines

### A couple who both work

When a couple both have jobs, they will share the work of running the home between them, in the way that suits them best. Perhaps one will cook the evening meal and the other will wash up afterwards. At the weekend perhaps one will wash and iron and the other will dust and vacuum. They might do the weekly shopping together.

The way in which they choose to divide the work doesn't matter. The important thing is to realize that both should have a fair share of work and leisure time.

### A woman at home all day

When a woman is at home all day, perhaps with small children, she will probably do most of the routine housework herself during the day. However, when babies are very small and when two- or three-year-olds are at the very energetic stage, they need constant attention. A mother may find that she has very little time to spare for extra housework in between cooking meals, washing up, shopping and washing clothes.

Her husband can help in various ways. When a baby is very young he can take turns in getting up when the baby wakes up at night. He can bath children and put them to bed in the evening. By taking part in their daily routine like this he will get to know his children better, as well as ensuring that both he and his wife have some leisure time in the evening.

### Labour-saving equipment

An automatic washing machine is a great time-saver in a family with children. With babies in the family the number of dirty nappies to be washed can seem endless. Babies may need several changes of clothes in a day, and small children playing on the floor or outside in the garden or yard can get very grubby very quickly. They may need clean, dry clothes at least once a day. Older children playing football or climbing trees or walls will add to the pile of washing. A washing machine is more of a necessity than a luxury in these circumstances, and non-iron clothes which can be machine-washed are the most sensible choice.

### Children helping at home

Children should be encouraged to be useful members of the family from an early age. Even small children can put toys away, and tidy their beds, especially if they have continental quilts. They can help clear and lay the table. Older children and teenagers can help with cooking, washing, cleaning, and shopping. They should all be able to iron their own shirts and press their own trousers.

If everyone helps in the running of the household then all the members of the family will realize that hot meals don't just appear on the table and that clean, ironed clothes don't just appear in the drawer.

If a housewife has always waited hand and foot on her family she cannot be surprised if they don't appreciate her work but take her effort for granted. Nor is she helping her children if they grow up incapable of looking after themselves when they leave home.

---

Questions

1  **Do you think it is a good idea to do the housework according to a routine? Why is this?**
2  **What are the factors which decide how much time you spend on housework every day?**
3  **Suggest a possible routine for a young couple with no children, who both leave for work at 8.30 a.m. and return about 5.30 p.m.**

# Cleaning routines

There are some jobs in the house which have to be done every day to keep the house looking tidy and clean. Other jobs should be done at least weekly, to keep the home thoroughly clean. There are extra household jobs too, which have to be fitted in when necessary.

How often you do these extra jobs, for example cleaning mirrors and windows, washing ornaments, washing curtains and walls, shampooing carpets and chairs, depends on you. Some people enjoy housework, others hate it, most people are somewhere in between. Everyone decides for himself or herself how important it is to them whether or not the furniture is always immaculately polished and completely free of dust. Often people would rather spend their spare time doing something they find more interesting and enjoyable.

It is important, however, to have high standards of cleanliness in the kitchen and bathroom, because these are areas where bacteria could thrive and cause illness. Nobody wants to eat food which has been prepared in a dirty kitchen, and nobody wants to use a bathroom or toilet which isn't clean.

To clean rooms thoroughly you should work in this order:

**Kitchen**

1 Open the window to air the room.
2 Thoroughly wash and dry the sink and draining-board.
3 Clean the cooker, including the oven. This is much easier if the cooker is wiped down each time it is used.
4 Wash work surfaces with hot, soapy water.
5 Defrost and clean the refrigerator.
6 Clean the larder or food cupboard.
7 Wipe the paintwork, cupboard doors and window sills.
8 Empty and wash the waste bin.
9 Sweep and wash the floor.

**Living-room**

1 Open the windows.
2 Clean and lay the coal fire if there is one.
3 Empty the ashtrays and waste-paper basket, remove old newspapers or dead flowers.
4 Tidy the room, straighten cushions.
5 Sweep or vacuum the carpet and surrounds.
6 Dust and polish the furniture.
7 Dust the skirting boards, wipe the paintwork with a damp cloth.
8 Vacuum or brush the chairs.

**Bedrooms**

1 Open the windows.
2 Tidy away clothes, toys and books.
3 Make the beds – everyone in the family should make their own bed.
4 Change the sheets when necessary.
5 Sweep or vacuum the carpet.
6 Dust and polish or wash the furniture.
7 Wipe the paintwork.

**Bathroom**

1 Open the window, straighten the towels.
2 Brush the W.C. with a special lavatory brush.
3 Wash the lavatory with a mild solution of disinfectant. You should keep a special cloth for cleaning the W.C. and not use it for any other job.
4 Encourage everyone to clean the bath straight after use, when it is much easier to do. Use a little detergent or a non-scratch cleaner which will not spoil the surface. Never use harsh scouring powder.
5 Clean the wash basin with the same cleaner. Rinse it well.
6 Wipe under and around the taps with a damp cloth, then rub them dry.
7 Wipe the window sill to remove dust.
8 Wash and dry the paintwork and tiles with detergent and warm water.
9 Wash the floor with disinfectant and warm water.

Questions

1 **List the cleaning jobs in (a) the kitchen, (b) the living-room, and (c) the bathroom, which you would try to do every day.**
2 **Which rooms in the house is it especially important to keep thoroughly clean, and why?**
3 **Make a list of the extra jobs around the house which you would do when you were spring-cleaning.**
4 **Suggest some household jobs which any teenagers in the family could do regularly.**

# Cleaning equipment and materials

It is a good idea to keep most of the items you use for cleaning together in one cupboard, away from cooking utensils or food. Always remember to keep polishes, bleaches and cleaners out of the reach of small children, as many of these everyday household items are poisonous if swallowed. Never transfer them into old lemonade bottles.

Having the right tools and cleaners makes it much easier to do a job well. You will need most of the following items for everyday cleaning:

*Equipment*
Hard broom (for outside)
Soft broom
Dustpan and brush
Upholstery brush
Vacuum cleaner (see page 100)
Attachments
Carpet sweeper
Mop, bucket
Dusters
Floorcloth
Cleaning rags
Chamois leather for windows

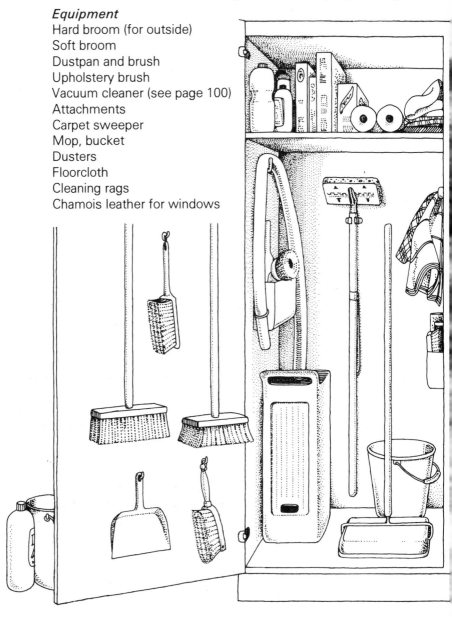

*Materials*
Polish for furniture and floors
Metal polishes – for silver, brass, copper
Cleaner for windows and mirrors
Liquid detergent (washing-up liquid)
Non-scratch cleaner for working surfaces, sink, cooker, etc.
Scouring powder
Soda for drains
Disinfectant for sinks, general cleaning
Bleach
Products for washing clothes (see page 114)

## Comparing different products

There is such a variety of cleaning products available in the shops that it is useful to compare them to find out which suits you best. You can buy furniture polish, for example, as a spray, a wax or a liquid. You can use a spray, a liquid, or warm water and a wash-leather to clean the windows.

Look at different products made for the same purpose and compare:

1 The cost of the bottle, aerosol or packet, and the quantity it contains.
2 How long you would expect it to last.
3 Which involves most effort, or hard rubbing?
4 Which gives the best results?
5 Does it have a pleasant smell?
6 Can it harm or scratch surfaces?
7 Can you use it for different cleaning jobs?

*Aerosols*
Many household cleaners and toiletries are available as aerosol sprays. Although they are easy and convenient to use, it is thought that some of the chemicals used to propel the contents out of the can are damaging the ozone layer around the earth – that is, the part of the earth's atmosphere which protects us from any harmful effect of the sun's rays.

---

Questions

1 **How can you avoid the danger of a child being accidentally poisoned in the home?**
2 **Look at the list of cleaning equipment and materials. Write a list of the items you would consider necessary for your own home.**
3 **What points would you look for in buying**
a **furniture polish**
b **a product for cleaning windows**
c **a product for cleaning kitchen work surfaces?**
4 **What are the advantages and disadvantages of using aerosol sprays?**

# Household pests

### Woodworm

Woodworm in houses is mainly caused by the furniture beetle, a small brown insect about 3 mm long. The beetle attacks dry timber such as the floor, stairs or furniture in a house, and lays eggs which develop into the 'woodworm'. The worm bores into the wood, feeding on it, for about three years, then tunnels its way out to mate.

Look carefully for the signs – small round holes and sawdust nearby – in house timber and old furniture. Liquids such as 'Rentokil' can be used to treat the wood and kill the beetle or worm, but where damage is extensive the infested wood may have to be cut out, burned and replaced with new treated timber.

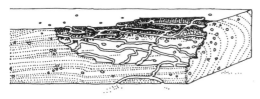

### Rodents

Rats and mice are a serious health hazard. They eat and spoil food, contaminating it with their droppings. They can carry fleas and spread disease and dirt.

Food must always be stored in closed containers or cupboards where it cannot attract rodents. Dustbins should have firmly fitting lids.

If you see any signs of rats or mice, such as droppings or food packets that have been gnawed, you should immediately get in touch with the Rodent Officer from your local council. He will help you get rid of the infestation with suitable poisons or traps.

### Fleas

Fleas can be brought into the house by cats and dogs. They lay eggs in carpets, furniture and house dust. Sprays and powders can be bought to treat them, and the local council will usually give help and advice on the best way to get rid of them.

### Flies

Flies can carry many serious diseases. They feed and lay eggs on food and decaying rubbish, moving from one to the other and spreading bacteria from their bodies. When eating they excrete a saliva which is mixed with the food, then sucked back into their mouths.

All food must be kept covered to discourage flies. Rubbish bins should be kept clean and firmly closed.

Flies can be killed by swatting, or by using an aerosol spray in a closed room with food covered. Another product is available which hangs in the room giving off a vapour poisonous to flies. This lasts for several months. However, it is thought that the vapour could be harmful to humans as well as flies.

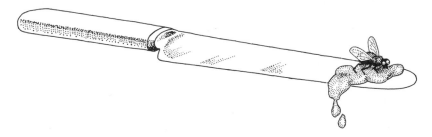

### Cockroaches

Cockroaches live in dark, warm, places – near hot pipes, ovens or boilers. They come out at night to look for food, spreading bacteria from their sticky bodies and infecting food with their droppings.

Food should be stored away from warm places, but if any infestation occurs, all dark corners should be thoroughly cleaned out and poisonous D.D.T. powder laid on the floor near skirtings and drains.

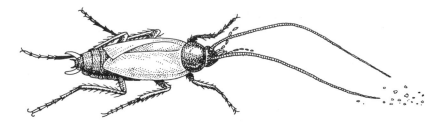

Questions

1 **List some hygiene rules every householder should follow to help prevent the infestation of any pests in the home.**
2 **What steps would you take to get rid of the following from an old house:**
a **rats and mice**
b **fleas**
c **cockroaches?**
3 **What would you consider to be the safest way of killing flies in your kitchen?**

# Further work on chapter 4

1   A young couple are setting up home. What do you consider should influence their choice of furniture?

2   Plan a study-bedroom for a teenage schoolgirl. Illustrate your answer with a large, clear, labelled diagram. Show how you would ensure adequate lighting and suggest with reasons a suitable type of carpet for the room. (O)

3   Draw up and display a detailed scheme for decorating and furnishing the living-room of a home of your own.

Collect samples of the carpet, curtains, cushion covers, wallpaper and paint, giving prices of each. Show illustrations of the furniture, lamps and other accessories you would like, giving the cost of these. Work out approximately the total cost of your scheme.

4   (a) What points would you consider when buying furniture for a small house?
(b) Draw a diagram to show the position of the furniture in an L-shaped lounge/dining-room where the dining area faces north. (Indicate the colour scheme.)
(c) State the materials from which the furniture and soft furnishings are made. (WMEB)

5   Collect and display samples of as many different types of carpets and floor coverings as you can. Give a description of each one, including the approximate price per square metre.

6   Give four points which must be considered when purchasing material for curtains for a family living-room. (O)

7   List all the items you would need for fully equipping a single bed with (a) traditional bedding, and (b) a continental quilt.
Find out the cost of each item on the list and compare the overall cost. Say which you would prefer to buy if you were setting up home, with your reasons.

8   Name two household pests most likely to be found in an old house. Account for their presence and give instructions for their control and elimination. (O)

---

**Books for further reading**

*Home Management and House Care* **Emily Carpenter** Heinemann Educational
*Running a Home is Fun* **Good Housekeeping Institute** Ebury Press
*At Home with Science* **O. F. G. Kilgour** Heinemann Educational
*Hygiene in the Home* **Elisabeth Norton** Mills and Boon

# Chapter 5
# The kitchen

# Kitchen planning

The more efficiently a kitchen is planned and laid out, the less energy the person working there has to waste walking from one part to another.

Most work in the kitchen involves food and is carried out in this order: storage → preparation → washing → cooking → serving.

The equipment used for this work is as follows:
cupboard or refrigerator → work surface → sink → cooker → work surface.

This equipment should be placed as close as possible to cut down unnecessary walking from one item to another.

It is best to place the three main areas – sink, cooker and storage – at the three points of a triangle, not more than 7 metres apart, and linked by work surfaces. The sink and cooker should each have a work surface on both sides. Storage of food and utensils in everyday use is best provided by wall cupboards above the work surface and a refrigerator below.

This could give either of these two basic layouts which are both convenient and energy saving.

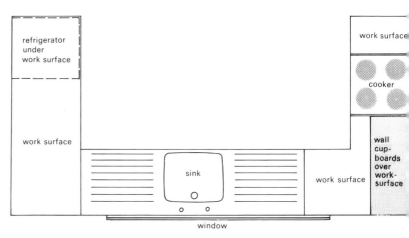

U-shape

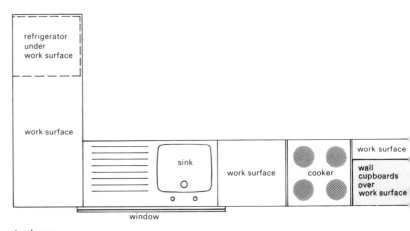

L-shape

Once the position of these items of equipment has been settled, other items such as a washing machine, breakfast bar or table and chairs can be fitted in.

*Work surfaces* should be made of hard, easily-cleaned, heat- and stain-resistant material. Plastic laminates such as Formica and Melamine are ideal. You should clean them by washing them with hot water and liquid detergent, and remove marks with a non-scratch cleaner.

*Floors* should be easy to clean, hard-wearing, attractive, and resistant to heat, grease and water. They should not be slippery, but warm, comfortable and not too noisy to walk on. Good quality vinyl is a good choice. Other suitable coverings are linoleum, cork or quarry tiles.

*Walls* must be easy to clean as they have to withstand a lot of steam and grease. A splash-back made of ceramic tiles behind the sink and cooker is useful. Suitable wall coverings are gloss or emulsion paint, washable or vinyl wallpapers, tiles, or wood panels treated with a seal.

*Curtains* should be easy to wash and iron. If the window is near the cooker, avoid curtains which could blow on to the flame and catch fire. Venetian or roller blinds are suitable as long as they are washable.

*Lighting* in a kitchen should be good. Daylight is best whenever possible. Fluorescent strip lighting is ideal as it casts no shadows. Though a little more expensive to install than ordinary lighting it costs less to run.

*The kitchen sink* may have one or two draining-boards and sometimes a double sink compartment. It may be made of:

1 Stainless steel – hard-wearing, easy to keep clean, but expensive.
2 Vitreous enamel – less expensive. It will wear well provided you avoid clashing it with metal pans or utensils.
3 Fireclay sinks – fairly hard-wearing, but not installed in new houses now except as an extra sink for laundry. The join between the sink and wooden draining-board could harbour dirt and bacteria. The modern one-piece sink and draining-board is more hygienic and easier to clean.
4 Plastic or fibre-glass sinks. These are not hard-wearing enough for everyday use, but are adequate for occasional use – in a caravan, for example.

---

Questions

1 **Why is it important to have a well-planned kitchen?**
2 **What is the usual order of handling food when preparing a meal?**
3 **What are the main work areas involved in preparing a meal?**
4 **What three areas in the kitchen should be at the three points of an imaginary triangle?**
5 **Draw a diagram of a well-planned kitchen which has room for meals to be eaten.**
6 **What are the main points to consider when choosing each of the following for a kitchen: work surfaces, floor-covering, wall-coverings, curtains, lighting and sink unit?**

# Cookers

**The gas cooker**

Gas cookers are more easily and quickly controlled than electric cookers although they are not as clean in use. They are usually fitted with castors and a flexible pipe so that they can be pulled away from the wall for easy cleaning and decorating.

A cooker is made up of three main parts: the hob (or hotplate), the grill and the oven.

### The hob

The hob usually has four burners. These may vary in size — smaller for simmering and larger for fast boiling. The burners on a modern cooker are lighted either automatically or by a push button. The hob may be sealed to prevent leakage of spilled food or it may be removable for easy cleaning at the sink. It should be cleaned with a damp cloth straight after use, and a non-scratch cleaner or soaped steel-wool pad can be used if necessary.

### The grill

The grill is usually at eye-level. Some grills have attachments for spit-roasting.

### The oven

1  The temperature in a gas oven varies slightly. The setting on the control relates to the centre of the oven. The top will be rather hotter, the bottom cooler, so that dishes needing slightly different temperatures can be cooked at the same time.

2  Modern ovens have a flame failure device which cuts off the supply of gas if the flame accidentally goes out.

3  Automatic controls are built into many gas cookers to switch the oven on and off at any time you set. If you go out it can switch itself on, cook the meal for your return and switch off. A minute-timer and kitchen clock are built in with these controls.

4  Oven linings may be non-stick, or may have a special finish which cleans itself continuously while the oven is on.

5  A removable drop-down door and oven roof may be fitted to make cleaning easier.

6  A light or inner glass door may be fitted so that you can see how food is cooking, without opening the door and possibly spoiling the food.


**Electric cookers**

These are cleaner to use than gas but are less easy to control quickly.

### The hotplate

The hotplate may have three or four rings. One of these may be particularly fast to heat, or a ring may have a thermostatic control to keep food just simmering. Some rings may be switched only half on, enough to heat a small pan economically. Controls should be out of the reach of children.

A ceramic hob has the rings fitted inside one smooth sheet of glass ceramic. The surface is very smooth and easy to clean and is not easily scratched or stained.

*The grill*

The grill is sometimes part of a smaller second oven. For economy, some grills can be switched on at one side only.

*The oven*

The oven in an electric cooker has a very even temperature.

1   A fan-assisted oven has an electric fan which circulates the warm air. This heats the oven more quickly and economically, and cooks the food on each shelf evenly. The fan can, however, be rather noisy in use.

2   Automatic controls similar to those in a gas cooker can be built in.

3   Some ovens have linings which clean themselves continuously in the same way as those in gas cookers. Other electric cookers have ovens which can be heated to a very high temperature while the door is locked. All the grease and dirt inside the oven is turned to ash which can easily be swept away when the oven cools.

## Microwave cookers

Microwave cookers will cook and reheat food in a fraction of the time taken by conventional cookers. For example, a baked jacket potato will cook in eight minutes. Because of this speed, microwave cookers are becoming quite widely used in homes as well as in catering establishments. They are simple to use and install as they are just plugged into a 13-amp socket outlet. As they require only a short time for cooking, they are very economical with fuel.

Microwave cookers contain a magnetron which produces microwaves. Food is cooked by energy produced by the vibration of these microwaves. Materials with a high water content, like most foods, absorb the microwave energy and this causes a rise in the temperature of the food.

Microwave cookers do not replace the conventional gas or electric cooker, as they do not do all the tasks that these cookers do, but they can be a useful addition. If you buy a microwave cooker you will receive detailed instructions on how to use it. You can often find courses on microwave cookery which you can join, to give you ideas on making the best use of the cooker.

Questions

1   **Describe the ways in which the different parts of a gas cooker can be made easier to clean.**

2   **Which part of a gas oven is the hottest? Your teacher may be able to borrow a suitable thermometer to test this.**

3   **Automatic controls on a cooker make it more expensive to buy. What advantages do they have to make the extra cost worthwhile?**

4   **What is the main advantage of (a) a gas cooker, and (b) an electric cooker? Which would you buy for your own home? Give the reasons for your choice.**

5   **Describe two ways in which the oven in an electric cooker can be made easier to clean.**

6   **What are the advantages of microwave cookers? How do they cook food?**

# Refrigerators and freezers

### Refrigerators

Refrigerators are ideal for storing food. They are useful because:
1. They provide a cold, airtight compartment to keep food fresh and clean. The bacteria which make food go bad are not very active at this low temperature, which is usually below 7°C.
2. You can go shopping much less often as you do not have to buy fresh food daily but can store it.
3. Left-over food can be kept fresh, so there is less waste.
4. You can keep a ready supply of frozen food in the special storage compartment; as a stand-by for visitors, for when you do not have time to prepare a meal or for when you run out of food.
5. Some foods, such as cold puddings, milk, or fruit juice taste much nicer when served really cold.

### How a refrigerator works

Refrigerators work on the principle that when liquids evaporate and turn to vapour (gas), they absorb heat to do this.

If you spill nail varnish remover or petrol on your hand it will absorb warmth from your skin to evaporate, making your hand feel cold.

A special liquid in the frozen food compartment evaporates, taking heat from the food in the fridge to do this. In this way, the food becomes cold As the vapour cools it turns back to a liquid and again absorbs heat from the fridge. This cycle goes on continuously, keeping the food constantly cold.

### How to use a refrigerator

1 Store food in the most suitable position. The part nearest the frozen food compartment is coldest, the door is the least cold.
2 Cover food before placing in the fridge, to prevent it from drying out.
3 Never put hot food into a fridge, as it will raise the temperature.
4 Do not open the door unnecessarily.
5 Arrange food on the shelves so that cold air can circulate freely.
6 When going on holiday empty the fridge, switch it off and open the door.
7 Never refrigerate bananas (they go black), root vegetables or apples.
8 Wrap strong-smelling foods well, or other foods may absorb their smell.

### How to look after your refrigerator

*Defrost* it regularly, as soon as the ice on the freezing compartment is as thick as a pencil. Defrosting may be:
*Fully automatic* – it may switch off, defrost and switch back on whenever necessary, completely automatically.
*Semi-automatic* – a push-button is pressed when you wish to defrost. When defrosting is complete it switches itself on again.
*Manual* – you switch off, remove the food and wrap any frozen food in several layers of newspaper to keep it cool. Defrosting can be speeded up by placing a bowl of hot water in the freezing compartment. When all the ice has melted into the drip tray, this can be emptied and replaced. Wipe out the fridge and dry it, replace the food and switch on.

*Cleaning.* Wash the inside of the refrigerator with a solution of one tablespoon of bicarbonate of soda to one pint of warm water. Do not use detergent as the smell may linger and affect the food. The outside can be washed with hot, soapy water and dried with a soft cloth. A little furniture cream should be used occasionally on the outside, to keep it in good condition.

### How to choose a refrigerator

1 Choose one large enough to suit your family, or a little larger.
2 Make sure it will fit into the space available.
3 Consider the way in which it has to be defrosted.
4 Some refrigerators are combined with a separate small freezer (page 96).
5 Frozen food compartments have star markings which are a guide to their temperature and so to the length of time ready-frozen foods can be safely stored in them.

    ❄ The temperature is about −6° C.
      Food can be stored up to one week.

    ❄❄ The temperature is about −12° C.
      Food can be stored up to one month.

    ❄❄❄ The temperature is about −18° C.
      Food can be stored up to three months.

    These frozen food compartments are for the storage of ready-frozen foods, they are not for freezing fresh foods. They are not cold enough to do this safely unless they have this extra star marking: ❄❄❄❄

## Freezers

A freezer is designed to freeze fresh food and keep it at or below −18°C for long periods without spoilage.

Freezers have the following advantages:

1   You can have a good store of food always available, particularly if you live a long way from the shops.
2   If you have a large garden you can freeze your own fruit and vegetables for use later in the year.
3   You can buy fruit and vegetables when they are in season and at their best and cheapest.
4   You can 'batch-bake', preparing several dishes at one baking session and freezing those you do not need straight away.
5   Ready-frozen foods can be bought in bulk from supermarkets or 'freezer centres' at lower prices than normal.
6   Freezers are useful when cooking for a party as dishes can be prepared in advance, saving a last minute rush.

These disadvantages must also be considered:

1   The cost of buying and running the freezer. It will use about 1½–2 units of electricity for each cubic foot of space per week (1 unit per 1.5 litres).
2   The cost and time involved in preparing and packaging foods.
3   The possibility of food spoilage during a power cut, or the cost of insurance against this.
4   The cost of servicing or repair.
5   The space the freezer will occupy.

## Types of freezer

*Chest type.* Top-opening lid, a little cheaper to buy and run.

*Upright type.* Front-opening door, easy to pack and unpack and to check food stocks. Uses less floor space.

*Fridge/freezer.* Combines an upright freezer with a refrigerator in one cabinet. Useful where space is limited.

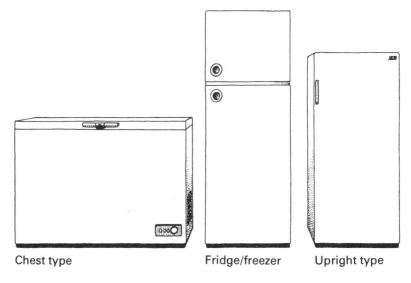

Chest type          Fridge/freezer          Upright type

### Some rules for freezing food

1  Only freeze food which is in perfect condition.
2  Never re-freeze food once it has thawed. Bacteria increase rapidly in food which has previously been frozen.
3  All meat and poultry must be completely thawed before cooking.
4  Foods which freeze well: pastry, bread, cakes, meat, soups, stews and vegetables.
5  Some foods do not freeze well. These include salad vegetables, milk, bacon, eggs in shells, large fruits unless cooked (e.g. stewed apple).
6  Foods must be properly packaged and labelled.
7  Store food only for the recommended time.
8  Never put warm food in the freezer.
9  Open the freezer as little as possible.
10 Defrost the freezer regularly, according to the manufacturer's instructions.
11 When adding more than 1 kg of fresh food to the freezer, set the control to 'fast freeze'. This prevents the temperature from rising and causing food spoilage.

### Packaging frozen foods

This must be carried out carefully, or foods may dry out and odours pass from one food to another.

Suitable materials: heavy-duty polythene bags, sheets of polythene for large, awkward shapes such as a turkey, plastic containers, foil and foil dishes. Special freezer tape and wire twists are suitable for closing bags.

All food should be clearly marked with the date and contents. It is useful to keep a book recording what you put in and take out of the freezer so that you know exactly what you have in stock.

Questions

1  **List six advantages of having a refrigerator.**
2  **Describe briefly how a refrigerator works.**
3  **Draw a diagram showing where in the fridge you would store: eggs, lard, fish-cakes, uncooked meat, a packet of frozen peas.**
4  **How should you cover the following before putting them into a fridge? (a) some Cheddar cheese, (b) a joint of meat, (c) some herrings, (d) slices of corned beef.**
5  **How often should you defrost a fridge? Describe how you would defrost it manually and thoroughly clean it.**
6  **Draw the four different star symbols found in refrigerators. Say what each means.**
7  **What do you consider would be the four main advantages to you of having a freezer?**
8  **List six costs involved in having a freezer.**
9  **What are the three main types of freezer? Give some points for and against each one.**
10 **Give the general rules you should follow when freezing food.**
11 **Name eight foods which it would be useful to have in store in your freezer. How would you pack and label each one?**

# Dishwashers

Hundreds of hours are spent yearly, in every household, washing up after meals. A dishwasher can do this job for you, efficiently and hygienically. It is particularly useful in a large family or for a household which has a lot of visitors.

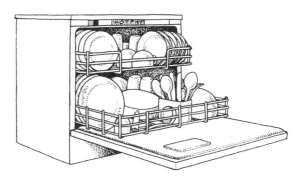

### Sizes

There are different types and sizes available to suit the needs of most families. You can have one built into a fitted kitchen, or placed on top of a work-bench, or you can have a free standing model. The size is measured by the number of place settings it will hold, usually between four and twelve.

### Plumbing

Dishwashers can often be plumbed directly into the hot or cold water supply and as the cycle may take any time between about 20 and 90 minutes it is an advantage to have this done, so that the taps at the sink are free for normal use.

### Hygiene

The dishwasher is often used only once a day. Dirty plates and utensils are stacked inside until it is full, then the day's washing-up is done all at once. The standard of hygiene is high, as a special detergent is used and the water is hotter than you could use at the sink. Because of this, however, hand-painted china, very fine glass and cutlery with glued-on handles should not be placed in the machine. Most everyday articles are quite safe.

### How it works

The dishwasher works by forcing a spray or jet of water around the dishes inside the machine. The pressure behind the water may be adjustable according to whether very dirty pans or fairly clean plates are being washed.

As the normal washing-up after a meal includes china, glasses, cutlery and saucepans you want a machine which will give good overall results when loaded with a variety of different items.

## Disadvantages

Although a dishwasher can be useful and labour-saving it does have disadvantages which should be considered if you are thinking of buying one.

1  The high cost which tends to make us think of dishwashers as a luxury rather than a necessity.
2  The cost of servicing and repair, to keep the dishwasher in good working order.
3  The cost of the special detergent and rinsing solution which are recommended for the best results.
4  The cost of having the machine plumbed in or else the inconvenience of having the taps unavailable for about an hour while the machine completes its cycle.
5  The time involved in rinsing all food scraps off plates or saucepans before they can be loaded.
6  The time and effort involved in loading and unloading the machine; unless there is a great deal of washing-up to be done it may be simpler and quicker to do it by hand in a bowl at the sink.
7  If you planned to run the machine only once a day, you might need to buy extra crockery and cutlery to last the day.
8  A dishwasher will use about one unit of electricity to wash the dinner dishes for a family of four.

## To help you choose

When you are choosing any expensive household appliance it is important to find out as much as you can about the different kinds available. You can do this by:

a  looking for information in the magazine 'Which?' (see page 136)
b  asking for advice from your local Consumer Advice Centre.
c  talking to friends who have one.
d  studying the manufacturers' leaflets and instruction booklets.

Questions

1  **Name two kinds of household where a dishwasher might be very useful.**
2  **Describe a family who would probably find it simpler and easier to do their washing-up by hand.**
3  **Why is it best to have a dishwasher plumbed in?**
4  **What are the disadvantages of having a dishwasher?**
5  **List the different ways of finding information about different models, to help you choose between them.**
6  **Name three kinds of shops where you could go to look at different dishwashers.**
7  **List these household appliances in the order in which you would save up to buy them, if you had a limited amount of money to set up home: vacuum cleaner, cooker, dishwasher, waste disposal unit, washing machine, electric food-mixer, refrigerator, split-level cooker.**

# Vacuum cleaners

## How vacuum cleaners work

A vacuum cleaner is an efficient way of cleaning as it collects dust and dirt and does not just move it from one place to another. A motor blows air out of the cleaner. This creates a vacuum. Air is sucked into the vacuum to replace the air blown out, and the dust and dirt are sucked in with the air. The dirt is collected either in a cloth bag which is later emptied, or in a disposable paper bag which can be thrown away and replaced. Although disposable bags are cleaner to use, the cost of buying them has to be considered. The bag should never be allowed to get more than half-full, or it will not work efficiently. For one unit of electricity you can do between two and four hours' cleaning.

## Types of vacuum cleaner

### Cylinder type

With this kind it is easier to get into awkward corners and under low furniture. It has to be put together when you want to use it and taken to pieces when you have finished with it, but this does not take long. This kind can be used for cleaning lino, vynolay or polished wooden floors and is quicker and better than sweeping them with a brush.

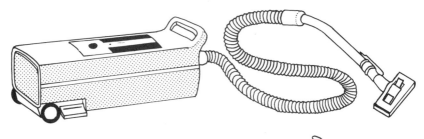

### Upright type

This is quicker for large areas of carpet. It beats the carpet as it cleans it, which loosens the dirt and makes it easier to pick up. There is a brush underneath which picks up threads which would otherwise stick to the carpet. These threads should be removed from the brush when you finish cleaning. Usually the handle can be lowered to make it possible to reach under low furniture.

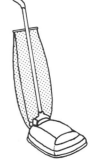

Attachments may be fitted to both types of cleaner, for dusting, for upholstery or curtains or for cleaning down the sides of armchairs where it is difficult to reach.

## Carpet sweepers

These are useful for brushing over the carpet in between vacuuming. They pick up threads and crumbs very efficiently though they do not clean dust and dirt from down in the pile of the carpet.

When choosing a sweeper try to test it before you buy. Some models are much more efficient than others. Look for one whose handle stays upright and does not fall to the floor. A very small sweeper will have to be emptied frequently; a very lightweight one may spill fluff on to the floor.

## Electric scrubber/polisher

This is invaluable if you have a lot of polished wood or lino floors. It will save you a lot of hard work. It has stiff brushes which rotate to scrub the floor and soft pads to attach beneath the brushes when you want to use it for polishing.

### Shampooer

Some electric polishers can be used for shampooing carpets. They have a shampoo container and special shampooing brushes.

## Dustette

A dustette is a very small, lightweight vacuum cleaner, which can easily be carried in the hand. It is useful for cleaning the stairs, or for cleaning inside a car.

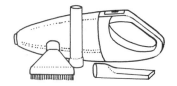

Questions

1 **What are the advantages and disadvantages of:**
a **a cylinder-type vacuum cleaner**
b **an upright vacuum cleaner?**
 **Which kind would you prefer for your own home?**
2 **List the different cleaning jobs which could be done with the attachments on a vacuum cleaner.**
3 **What points would you look out for when buying a carpet sweeper?**
4 **Why is an electric scrubber/shampooer/polisher useful? List the different brushes and pads which can be fitted to it.**
5 **List four cleaning jobs for which a dustette would be useful.**

# Small kitchen equipment

**The pressure cooker**

The pressure cooker works on the principle that when the pressure inside the pan is increased by preventing the escape of steam, a higher temperature is produced which cooks food in a shorter time.

*Advantages of having a pressure cooker*

1 *Speed.* Food can be cooked very quickly, in one-quarter to one-third of the usual cooking time. For example, a stew which would normally take two hours can be cooked in about twenty-five minutes, and potatoes can be cooked in six minutes.

2 *Fuel* can be saved, as food takes less time to cook, and as several foods can be cooked in the pan at the same time – for example, meat, potatoes and vegetables.

3 *The nutritive value* of food is high. Vegetables are cooked quickly and in steam rather than water, so there is a smaller loss of vitamins into the water.

4 *Cheaper, tougher cuts of meat*, which would otherwise take a long time to cook, can be pressure-cooked quickly and easily until tender.

5 *Different uses.* The cooker can be used for bottling fruit and vegetables to preserve them, for sterilizing baby's bottles, for making jam and marmalade, and for making baby foods.

*How to use a pressure cooker*

1 Study and follow the instruction book carefully, to gain confidence in controlling the cooker.

2 Do not overfill. The pressure cooker should be no more than half-full for liquids, two-thirds for solids.

3 Put the lid on, and place the cooker over high heat till a steady flow of steam comes through the vent. Add the weight which controls the amount of pressure in the cooker.

4 When a loud hiss is heard, start to time the food. Turn the heat down so that the cooker keeps up just a steady hiss.

5 Time food carefully, and do not overcook.

6 Cool either by leaving for about 5 to 10 minutes, or by running the cooker under cold water for a couple of minutes to reduce the pressure.

7 When the hissing stops, the control weight and lid may be removed.

### How to care for a pressure cooker

As it is usually made of polished aluminium it should be washed in hot, soapy water, dried well and stored with the lid off. Check that the rubber gasket is clean and replace it when it lets steam escape. The cooker can be sent to the makers every five years or so for servicing.

The cost is fairly high, but the pan is strong and well made and should last for many years. Look around and compare prices before you buy.

## Saucepans

Consider the following points when choosing from the wide variety available:

1   Heavier pans will spread heat more evenly and keep their shape better.
2   The pan should not be too heavy to lift easily.
3   Handles should be heat-resistant and firmly fixed.
4   Lids should fit well.
5   All pans used on electric cookers should have a heavy base.

### Metals used to make saucepans

*Aluminium.* Probably the most widely used. It is available in different thicknesses. Fairly thick aluminium pans are strong, long-lasting, easy to clean and reasonably priced. They should give good service for many years.

*Vitreous enamel on steel.* Look for this sign as a guide to quality. These pans are often chosen for their very attractive patterns and colours, which make them a good choice for oven-to-table ware. They need more care in use than aluminium pans as the enamel may become scratched or discoloured. Never use metal utensils or scouring powder on them.

registered trade marks
of the Vitreous Enamel
Development Council Ltd

*Enamel pans* are cheap, but lightweight and easily chipped. They may be satisfactory for foods such as vegetables which do not easily stick.

*Stainless Steel* is very expensive, but hard and strong. Pans tend to be thin because of the cost, so they often have a heavy base of aluminium or copper added, to spread heat evenly and prevent sticking. Wash them in hot, soapy water, and dry them straight away to prevent them becoming marked.

*Non-stick finish* is a coating of P.F.T.E., a plastic which may be applied to pans, baking tins and oven linings, to make them much easier to wash. If it is of good quality it should last quite well provided that you avoid scratching it. Never use metal utensils or metal pan cleaners in it, and never use scouring powder. A wash with hot, soapy water should be all that is needed. When used in baking tins it helps cakes to be more easily removed from the tin, though tins should still be lightly greased.

## Small electrical appliances

### Mixers

Mixers vary in power from a full-sized mixer with a large bowl and stand to smaller hand-mixers. They do not use much electricity, so they are quite cheap to run – one unit is enough for over sixty cakes to be mixed.

Mixers can be used for a variety of jobs: creaming cake mixtures, rubbing fat into flour, whipping cream or egg whites. Some larger models have a dough hook for kneading dough.

The mixer should be kept ready for use on a work bench. If it is put away in a cupboard you are less likely to use it often. Covers can be bought or made to keep it free from dust. Hand-mixers usually have a bracket for fixing them to the wall in a convenient place.

Attachments may be bought for some mixers to do a variety of jobs — slicing and shredding vegetables, extracting juice, grinding coffee beans, peeling vegetables, mincing meat. Provided they are strongly made and easy to attach and clean, attachments can be quick and labour-saving.

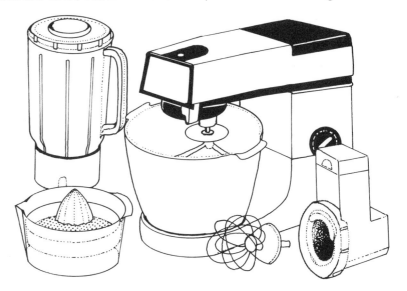

### Blenders

Blenders (or liquidizers) are very useful. They sometimes come as attachments to mixers or they may be bought separately. They are ideal for blending soups, making a puree of fruit or vegetables, chopping nuts, making crumbs from bread, biscuits or cakes and making baby foods.

They are inexpensive to run — one unit of electricity would blend about 500 pints of soup.

The blender should be used carefully, following the manufacturer's instructions. It should not normally be run for long periods as the motor may overheat. The best way to clean the goblet is to rinse off most of the food particles under the tap, half fill with warm water, add a drop of detergent and put the lid on. Switch on for a few seconds, rinse and dry. Unplug the motor and wipe with a damp cloth.

Never put the motor unit into the water.

### Toasters

It is more economical to use a toaster than to heat a grill just to make toast. One unit of electricity will toast about 70 slices of bread. Automatic 'pop-up' toasters will prevent toast burning. Some can toast up to four slices, lightly or well done.

You should never poke with a metal knife to loosen toast while the toaster is still plugged in, as this could give you an electric shock.

### Slow cooker

This is a large, well-insulated pan which can be plugged in, switched on and left to cook slowly all day. You could start a stew cooking in the morning, go out, and return to a hot, well-cooked meal. The cooker is well sealed to keep in moisture and flavour and is ideal for the long, slow cooking of inexpensive, tougher cuts of meat. It is quite economical, using only about the same amount of electricity as a light bulb.

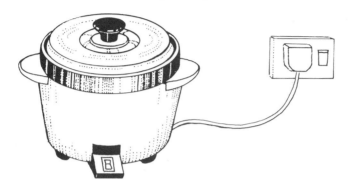

### Food processors

Food processors will process food in a variety of different ways without your having to buy any extra accessories. They will mix, cream fat and sugar, rub fat into flour, blend, mince, chop, slice, shred and knead. They perform all these operations very quickly, faster than a food mixer.

However, as they are not able to take large quantities at one time, they are not necessarily more useful than a mixer. Whether they are a better buy for you than a mixer depends upon the kind of food preparation you do most. If you do a lot of slicing or shredding of vegetables, or make a lot of marmalade or chutney, or mince your own meat, then they could save you a lot of time. But if you want a mixer more for making cakes and kneading dough for bread, or if you want to bake large quantities in bulk, perhaps for a freezer, then an electric mixer, maybe with a blender and a slicer/shredder, would be a more useful buy for you.

You should always look for the B.E.A.B. (British Electrotechnical Approvals Board) sign on any electrical appliance you are thinking of buying. (See page 20.)

---

### Questions

1 **What are the advantages of using a pressure cooker?**
2 **What important points should you look for when choosing pans?**
3 **Name three metals used to make saucepans, giving the points for and against each.**
4 **How should you look after pans, baking tins or oven-linings with a non-stick finish?**
5 **Name the three small electrical appliances you would most like in your kitchen. How would each be useful and how would you use and care for them?**

# Further work on chapter 5

1　A young couple have just moved into an unfurnished flat. Draw a clear labelled diagram of a kitchen which you think would suit them. How does your plan save time and energy? What kind of lighting should they choose for the kitchen? Give reasons. (O)

2　You have been asked for advice by a friend who is planning to renew her kitchen. Using graph paper, draw a scale plan of the kitchen showing doors and windows. Find out the sizes of sink units, cupboards, a cooker, washing machine and refrigerator, and plan a fitted kitchen for her.

3　Hygienic Sinks
(a) Name three types of material that can be used for making sinks and state one advantage and one disadvantage of each.
(b) Choose one type of sink and explain how you would keep it clean and hygienic.
(c) State the correct method of washing up after a dinner.
(d) How should you keep a dishcloth hygienic? (SEREB)

4　Find the average cost of each of the following items:
Cooker
Twin-tub washing machine
Automatic washing machine
Refrigerator
Chest-type freezer
Upright freezer
Dishwasher
Sink unit with cupboards below
Wall cupboard
Vacuum cleaner (cylinder)

5　(a) Make a plan of a kitchen to show the most suitable position of the following:
sink
cooker
refrigerator
window
automatic washing machine
two working surfaces
two doors
(b) Give reasons for the positioning of the following:
sink
cooker
refrigerator
automatic washing machine
working surfaces
(c) Suggest with reasons: (i) a suitable floor covering for your kitchen,
(ii) a suitable finish for the walls. (EMREB)

6 A kitchen needs much thought and care to be equipped successfully. What are the important points to consider in relation to each of the following:
(a) Sink and draining board
(b) Floor covering
(c) Storage of perishable foods
(d) Lighting

7 (a) Many housewives might consider the following items to be luxuries; state one point about each to justify the cost:
(i) household rubber gloves (ii) 'J' cloths (iii) roasting bags
(iv) absorbent kitchen roll (v) washing-up liquid.
(b) Give two facts about each of the following to explain its value:
(i) a liquidizer (ii) a home freezer (iii) a pressure cooker.
(c) List four points a working housewife should consider when choosing a new cooker. (ALSEB)

8 Freezing is a method of preserving food which is increasing in popularity. Prepare a project on methods used to preserve food in other times and in other places.

9 Deep freezing is a safe way of preserving food and the housewife is using this method of preparation nowadays.
(a) Give two advantages for buying each of the following types of freezer: (i) top-opening (ii) front-opening (iii) combined with refrigerator.
(b) Name three packaging materials which can be used in a freezer and give an example of one food suitable for packing in each material.
(c) List four points which will ensure successful home-freezing.
(d) What advantages would be enjoyed by a family which possessed a deep-freeze?

10 Two friends are spending Bank Holiday weekend with you (Saturday, Sunday, Monday). There is little time during the week to prepare for their visit but as you have a freezer much of the cooking can be done during the previous weekend.
(a) List four dishes you could prepare and freeze.
(b) Choose any two of these dishes and explain how they are made (recipes not required) and how you would pack them for the freezer. Describe what you would do to these dishes when required.
(c) How would you make the bedroom ready for your guests? (ALSEB)

11 Give one advantage for having each of the following in the home:
(a) a pressure cooker
(b) a silicone-lined pan
(c) an extractor fan
(d) an eye-level grill
(e) an automatic washing machine
(f) a cylinder vacuum cleaner

12   You are planning to buy: (i) a vacuum cleaner; (ii) a refrigerator; (iii) a pressure cooker.
(a) Using 'Which?' magazine (back copies in your local library) choose for each item a particular model you would like. Describe it fully, including its good and bad features.
(b) The same equipment is usually available at different prices in different places. Find out the manufacturer's recommended price for the items you have chosen, then find the cost of the same items in as many different places as you can, for example:
Electricity board showrooms
Department stores
Discount warehouses or shops
Electrical goods shops
Mail order catalogues.

13   Make a list of all the small equipment you would use in the kitchen for preparing meals (e.g. saucepans, cake tins, scales). Divide them into those you think are essential when first setting up home, and those you would add later when you could afford them.

Find out the cost of the equipment on your list.

14   Make a study of household equipment in the past, for washing, cooking, and cleaning, giving illustrations wherever possible. Try to arrange a visit to a museum where these items can be seen.

---

**Books for further reading**

*Cooking Explained* **Barbara Hammond** Longman
*The Kitchen* **Margaret Cullen** Heinemann Educational
*Science for Housecraft* **John Robinson** Edward Arnold
*Better Home Management* **Aileen King** Mills and Boon
*Running a Home is Fun* **Good Housekeeping Institute** Ebury Press
*Food Freezing at Home* **Gwen Conacher** Electricity Council
*A–Z of Cheaper Freezing* **Joan Hood** Home and Freezer Digest
*Antique Household Gadgets and Appliances* **David de Haan** Blandford Press

# Chapter 6
# The family washing

# Ways to do your washing

There are many different ways of coping with the family wash, from a bowl of hot, soapy water at the sink to an automatic electronic machine. The equipment you choose will probably depend on:

a   the money you have available

b   the size of your family

c   the time you can spend doing the washing.

Here are some of the ways you can get your washing done.

## The launderette

### Advantages

1   You do not have the cost of buying a machine.

2   They are quite cheap to use compared to the cost of buying, running and servicing your own.

3   Clothes can be washed and completely dried.

4   They are useful for large items such as blankets, even if you have a machine at home.

5   They are useful for drying clothes washed at home in wet weather, although some launderettes will not allow you to do this.

### Disadvantages

1   The time involved in getting to the launderette and waiting around for washing to be done is a disadvantage. Sometimes you can leave your washing in the care of an attendant and collect it later.

2   The results are not always very good, especially if you put different kinds of materials in the same wash-load to save expense.

## The laundry

The laundry will collect and deliver to your home. You parcel up the items to be washed, writing each item on a list. A laundry van calls once a week to collect them, returning them a week later, washed and ironed. There is a set charge for each article, depending on its size.

*Advantages*

1 There is no work involved for you. Your laundry is returned clean and well ironed.
2 If you are likely to be out when the van calls, you can take the laundry to a shop and collect it at a time which suits you.

*Disadvantages*

As each item is charged separately, it would be very expensive to do all the washing for a family this way; it could be useful, though, for items like sheets, towels and pillowcases, while clothes could be hand-washed at home, particularly if there are only one or two people.

## Washing by hand

This is hard work if there are more than a few small articles to be washed. It can be difficult to keep clothes a good colour, especially if they need very hot water. Hand washing is often best for delicate garments or fabrics. Pre-soaking in biological or other detergent makes hand washing easier, as does the use of a spin-drier.

## Washing by machine

You should consider the following points when choosing a machine:

1 The size, according to the size of your family. Size is measured by the weight of dry clothes the machine will hold, for example three kilos.
2 Does the machine have a built-in water heater? You may need one if you do not have a good supply of hot water.
3 Look for the B.E.A.B. label as a sign of safety.
4 Does the machine need a low-lather detergent?
5 Will it have to be plumbed-in to the water supply?
6 Find out all you can about a particular model you are thinking of buying. Ask friends, see if it has been tested by 'Which?', ask for information from your Consumer Advice Centre.
7 What type of machine do you want: automatic, twin tub, or a single tub with a wringer?

---

Questions

1 **Give as many reasons as you can why many people use launderettes to do their washing.**
2 **What are the points for and against sending some or all of your weekly washing to the laundry?**
3 **Describe two households where using a laundry for some or all of the washing would be suitable.**
4 **Make a list of all the clothes you can think of which would be best washed by hand.**
5 **You are helping a friend to choose a new washing machine. What do you think are the four most important points which she should consider carefully before spending her money?**

# Types of washing machine

### Single tub with a wringer

The wringer may be worked by hand or electricity. An electric wringer should have a safety device so that it can be quickly and easily knocked open if you get your fingers trapped.

The clothes may be washed either by the action of a paddle in the bottom of the tub (which is a slow, gentle action) or by a pulsator on the side of the tub. The action of the pulsator is quicker (perhaps four minutes instead of twelve to wash a load of clothes) but may be more likely to tangle the clothes. After the soapy water has been wrung out, the clothes are usually rinsed in the sink, then they are wrung again.

Twin tubs and automatics are becoming more popular than wringer machines. They are easier to use and extract more water from clothes than a wringer does.

### Twin tub

This has one tub for washing and another for rinsing and spin-drying. As in the single-tub machine the clothes are washed by the action of either a pulsator or a paddle. Some twin tubs have a continuous rinsing action in the spin-drier. This means that clean water can be fed into the spinner at the same time as soapy water is pumped out of it until the rinsing water runs clear. Most twin tubs have a heater and timer so that clothes can be washed at the correct temperature and for the correct length of time.

### Automatics

These have one tub for both washing and spinning. (Some more expensive models also tumble dry clothes in warm air in the same tub.) All you have to do with these machines is to put the clothes and detergent in, set the controls according to the water temperature, length of wash and length of spin required and switch on. The machine will wash, rinse and spin-dry without any help from you.

An automatic machine should be plumbed in to the water supply to leave the taps free while the machine is working. As these machines have more sophisticated controls than twin tubs they can be very expensive to repair if they go wrong.

An automatic will be either a 'front loader' or a 'top loader'.

### Front loader

1 Clothes are washed by a tumbling action in a revolving drum. This washing action is quite gentle, so that even delicate clothes can be washed safely.
2 Once it has started you can't open the door to add any more clothes.
3 A low-lather detergent must always be used – these are a little more expensive than others.
4 It takes up less kitchen space as it can be fitted under a work top.

### Top loader

1 This washes the clothes by the action of a paddle.
2 Clothes can be added after the wash has started.
3 Any washing powder may be used.
4 It uses more kitchen space as it cannot have a work top built over it.

Front loader    Top loader

## Which would you buy?

### Twin tub

Same hot soapy water washes several loads.
More time and work involved.
Can spin clothes very dry.

### Automatic

Hot water and detergent can be used for only one load.
No work involved, works automatically.
Does not usually spin quite so dry.
Should be plumbed in at extra cost.
May be more expensive to repair.

Prices of both types now tend to be similar.

---

### Questions

1 **How does a machine with a wringer get clothes clean? How would you rinse them?**
2 **How are the clothes in a twin tub with a pulsator washed and rinsed?**
3 **Describe the washing action in a front-loading machine.**
4 **If you were buying an automatic machine would you choose a front loader or a top loader? Give all your reasons.**
5 **You are trying to decide whether to buy a twin tub or an automatic. Give the advantages and disadvantages of both kinds.**

# Organizing your wash

### Preparing the clothes before washing

1  Mend any tears and darn any holes as they are likely to get bigger in the wash.
2  Make sure all pockets are empty. A paper handkerchief, for example, could disintegrate and spread fluff over the rest of the washing.
3  Always close zips, otherwise they may not close smoothly afterwards.
4  Tie any apron strings or tapes so they won't get tangled.
5  Remove any stains before washing or ironing (see page 120).
6  Sort clothes according to the colour and the fabric they are made from, or according to the wash code labels (see page 116).

### Which washing powder?

There are basically six different types of detergent for washing clothes. Each one is suitable for a particular purpose.

1  *Synthetic detergents,* e.g. Tide, Surf, Daz. These don't contain any soap. They are good for all general washing, by hand or machine (except front-loading automatics). They produce good lather even in hard water and are easy to rinse away.

2  *Soap powders* based on soap, e.g. Persil, Fairy Snow. They are made from natural animal or vegetable fats. They are good for all general washing by hand or machine, though in hard water areas they will not lather very well and may produce a scum.

3  *Biological (enzyme) detergents,* e.g. Radiant, Ariel, Biological Daz. These are synthetic detergents which contain enzymes to break down and remove protein stains such as milk, blood or egg. They are very useful for soaking out stains before washing. They work best in water which is hand-hot but not above 60°C.

Some fabrics – wool, silk and leather – should never be soaked. Garments with metal fasteners may not be suitable for soaking. Flame-resistant finishes should never be soaked but washed in hand-hot water.

Clothes which are not colour-fast should not be soaked. To test for colour fastness, wash an inconspicuous part of the garment in a washing powder solution and iron it while damp between two pieces of white fabric. If any colour comes out or if you are in doubt, wash the article quickly and separately, in warm water (40°C).

4  *Low-lather detergents,* e.g. Bold, Persil Automatic. Specially made to be used in front-loading automatic machines, they produce only a small amount of foam, as too much would prevent the machine from working efficiently.

5  *Grease-solvent washing powders,* e.g. Drive. These are specially formulated to remove greasy marks and stains from clothes, for example, greasy marks from cotton/polyester pillowcases or shirt collars, or oily marks from dirty overalls. They are also useful for soaking out stains such as butter or lard.

6  *Light duty detergents* e.g. Dreft, Stergene. These are suitable for hand-washing lightly soiled clothes or for delicate fabrics and wool. They are easy to rinse away and leave clothes feeling soft.

### Fabric Conditioners

These products – e.g. Comfort, Lenor – are not for cleaning clothes, but are added to the final rinsing water. They make clothes feel softer, add body to the fabric and reduce static electricity so that dirt is not attracted to the fabric. They give a soft, fluffy feel to wool, knitwear, towels and babies' nappies and leave clothes smelling nice.

### Hypochlorite bleach

Bleach, e.g. Domestos, is useful for keeping white cotton and linen a good white colour or for removing stains from them. It is strong and poisonous if swallowed and should only be used exactly in accordance with the makers' instructions. Keep bleach away from children and store it carefully.

### Starch

This gives a crisp, firm finish to cotton articles such as tablecloths, pillowcases, shirt collars and cuffs and it helps keep them clean for longer. It can be bought in powder or liquid form or as an aerosol spray which is convenient, quick and easy to use.

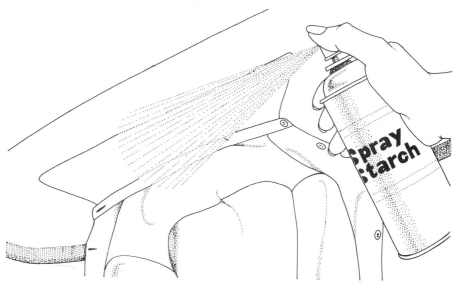

## Questions

1  **How would you prepare and sort clothes before washing?**
2  **Describe the different types of washing powder in everyday use in the home, saying when each would be a suitable choice.**
3  **How do fabric conditioners improve your washing results? Name some garments to which they give a particularly good finish.**
4  **Which fabrics can be safely treated with hypochlorite bleach?**
5  **What are the advantages of starching cotton garments after washing?**

# The H.L.C.C. labelling scheme

The Home Laundering Consultative Committee (H.L.C.C.) system of labelling clothes with washing instructions has been agreed between Britain and many other countries.

Nearly every garment you buy has a sewn-in label telling you exactly how to wash it to keep it in the best possible condition, according to the fabric it is made from. The labels give you the information listed below and should be followed carefully. A garment which is incorrectly washed just once can be completely spoiled and never restored to good condition.

1  The <u>temperature</u> of the water you should use. This may be:
100°C  Boiling
95°C  Very hot though not quite boiling
60°C  Hot – much too hot for the hands
50°C  Hand-hot – just as hot as your hands can stand
40°C  Warm – feels just warm to the touch
30°C  Cool – feels rather cool to the hands

2  Whether the garment should have a long or short machine wash, be hand-washed or not washed at all.

The length of time the garment should be machine-washed varies according to how delicate or strong it is, and is described on the label as <u>maximum</u>, <u>medium</u> or <u>minimum</u>.

3  Whether you can spin, wring, drip-dry or tumble-dry.

4  Whether you can use chlorine bleach (e.g. Domestos).

**May be treated with chlorine bleach**

**Do not use chlorine bleach**

5  The correct temperature for ironing.

Hot (210°C)
for cotton, linen, rayon

Warm (160°C)
for polyester mixtures, wool

Cool (120°C)
for acrylic, nylon, polyes

**Do not iron**

6  If and how the garment can be <u>dry cleaned</u>. The letter in the circle tells the dry cleaner which fluid to use.

**Do not dry clean**

## The wash code and how it is used

These labels are also found on most washing powder packets. If you know what fibre your garment is made from – and there is nearly always a label to tell you this sewn into it – you can follow the instructions and wash it correctly.

If you use an automatic, you just set your machine to the same washing process as the one on the label and the clothes will automatically have the correct programme.

If you use a twin tub or a single tub with wringer you follow the instructions under 'Machine wash'.

If you wash by hand, follow the instructions under 'Hand wash'.

All items with the same wash-code number can be safely washed together provided they are colour-fast.

*CARE LABEL* (handwritten)

 White cotton and linen articles without special finishes

 Cotton, linen or rayon articles without special finishes where colours are fast at 60°C

 White nylon; white polyester/cotton mixtures

 Coloured nylon; polyester; cotton and rayon articles with special finishes; acrylic/cotton mixtures; coloured polyester/cotton mixtures

Cotton, linen or rayon articles where colours are fast at 40°C, but not at 60°C

 Acrylics; acetate and triacetate, including mixtures with wool; polyester/wool blends

 Wool, including blankets, and wool mixtures with cotton or rayon; silk

 Silk and printed acetate fabrics with colours not fast at 40°C

 Cotton articles with special finishes capable of being boiled but requiring drip drying

Articles which must not be machine washed

 Do not wash

---

## Questions

1 **Why should you look for H.L.C.C. labels on the clothes you buy?**
2 **What are the water temperatures normally used for washing processes?**
3 **What do the terms <u>maximum</u>, <u>medium</u> and <u>minimum</u> mean when used on wash-care labels?**
4 **How would you wash and iron a woollen cardigan with this label?**

*- wool silk* (handwritten)    *no chlorine bleach   Warm   fluid you use when dry cleaning* (handwritten)

5 **How would you wash and iron a garment with this label?**

*Hot for cotton.   use Cl bleach   Hot Iron   Do not dry clean* (handwritten)

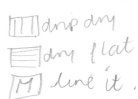 *drip dry   dry flat   line it.* (handwritten)

 *tumble drying* (handwritten)

# Drying and ironing

### Drying

Spin-driers extract most of the water from the clothes although they don't actually dry them. A spin-drier may be part of a twin tub or bought separately. Automatic machines also spin-dry clothes at the end of the cycle.

After clothes have been spun-dried or wrung they have to be completely dried. This can be done in any of the following ways:

1 *Drying outside on a line* gives clothes a soft texture and a fresh smell, is cheap and keeps moisture out of the house. The action of sunlight on white cotton keeps it a good colour, though wool should not be dried in the sun.

2 *A tumble-drier* can be used. Clothes which have been spun or wrung are tumbled in a revolving drum in a flow of warm air. You set the temperature of the air and the length of time in the drier according to whether you want the clothes just dry enough to iron or completely dry, and according to the fabric they are made from. It is important to set these controls correctly if you want good results.

A tumble-drier is especially useful for giving a soft, fluffy finish to towels and nappies. Pure wool garments should never be tumble-dried. Always follow the recommendations of the manufacturer.

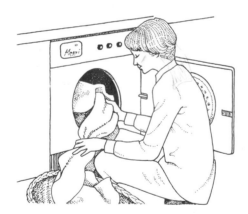

3 *Launderettes* have large-sized tumble-driers which you can sometimes use even if you wash the clothes at home.

4 *A pulley*, attached to the ceiling in a warm kitchen, is useful for drying and airing.

5 *A clothes-horse* will fold up when not in use. Some fit over the bath so that you can drip-dry clothes easily.

6 *Radiators* can be used, though clothes tend to become rather stiff and crumpled as they dry.

7 *Drying cupboards or cabinets* are less popular now for use in the home. Clothes are hung on rails or racks and warm air from a heater below dries them.

Whenever you have to dry washing indoors, by whatever method, make sure that the room is well ventilated to stop the air and walls from becoming damp

**Ironing**

Modern irons have a temperature control which can be set to the appropriate temperature for the fabric you are ironing. (See page 116.)

You can choose a dry or a steam iron. A dry iron is less expensive and can be used with a wet cloth for pressing or for very dry fabrics.

A steam iron is useful for ironing clothes which have become too dry. Other irons spray a fine jet of water over the clothes as they are being ironed. Both steam and spray irons can be used dry instead if you wish.

*Looking after the iron*

1 Stand the iron on its heel when you are not using it.
2 Don't wind the flex around the iron.
3 Clean the base of the iron with a steel-wool pad if it gets marked.
4 For a steam iron, it is best to use distilled water. This prevents the deposit of 'fur' which could block the steam vents.
5 Empty the water from the iron after use, while it is still hot.

Questions

1 **List six advantages of drying clothes outside.**
2 **Describe how you would use a tumble-drier.**
3 **Suggest five possible ways of getting your washing dry if it was too wet to hang it outside.**
4 **Give five points you would consider carefully before buying an iron.**
5 **How would you care for an iron to keep it in good condition?**

# Stain removal

Many everyday stains can be removed by treatment with ordinary washing powders. The treatment depends on:

a the type of stain
b the material which is stained.

1 The first rule with stains is to <u>act quickly</u> before the stain has time to set. Provided the article is washable you should:

a Put it into cold water (hot water will set the stain).
b Soak the article (unless unsuitable).
c Wash as usual.

2 *Removing stains by soaking*

a Most washing powders contain sodium perborate which removes stains such as tea, coffee or fruit juice. This acts both during soaking in hand-hot water (50°C) and during washing at a high temperature (95°C) if the fabric is suitable.
b An enzyme (biological) detergent will remove protein stains, e.g. blood, egg, milk or gravy, very effectively during a long soak in warm (40°C) water. After soaking rinse well, then wash in the normal way.

3 *Hypochlorite bleach,* e.g. Domestos, can be used to bleach stains out of white cotton or linen. Never use it undiluted and follow the instructions very carefully. Rinse carefully before washing.

4 *Grease-solvent washing powders* will remove many greasy marks during soaking and washing. outside to in

5 *Solvents,* e.g. turpentine, surgical spirit, trichlorethylene (Dabitoff) are used for stubborn greasy or oily stains, or on non-washable articles.
Place a clean white cloth below the stain. Soak another cloth in the solvent and dab at the stain, working from the outside in towards the centre. Rinse well then wash as usual. Air well, if not washable, to remove fumes, and only use solvents in a well-ventilated room.

## How to treat some common stains

*Blood, egg, milk, gravy* — Soak in a warm solution of biological detergent following instructions on the packet. Rinse well, then wash as usual, according to the fabric.

*Tea, coffee* — Soak in a hand-hot washing powder solution, then wash at the highest temperature suitable for the fabric. If the tea or coffee is milky, soak in a warm solution of biological detergent.

*Grass* — Treat with methylated spirits or another solvent. Rinse and wash well.
*Or* soak in biological detergent, rinse and wash.

*Ball-point pen* — Treat with methylated spirit or solvent, rinse and wash according to the fabric.

*Grease, oil, butter* — Soak and wash in grease-solvent washing powder. If not washable, treat with a solvent, and air.

*Chewing gum, tar* — Scrape off as much as possible, soften the stain by rubbing butter into it and then wipe off with a clean cloth. Remove remaining mark with a solvent then rinse and wash as usual.

*Unidentified stains* — These are best treated by a professional dry cleaner, if a cold rinse, warm soak and wash does not remove the stain.

## Dry cleaning

This is carried out by professional dry cleaners, or in a coin-operated machine at your launderette. It is used for all clothes which cannot be washed. A care-label inside the garment will often have a symbol to advise cleaners as to which particular fluid should be used for cleaning, or to advise against any dry cleaning.

---

Questions

1  **What are the two main considerations in deciding how to treat a stain?**
2  **If a cup of tea was spilt on a table-cloth, what immediate action would you take?**
3  **How can ordinary washing powders help remove stains?**
4  **What kind of stains do biological detergents remove?**
5  **How would you remove a stain from an article which could not be washed?**
6  **How would you remove the following stains:**
a  **gravy from a cotton table-cloth**
b  **butter or grease from a tea-towel**
c  **an unidentified stain on an overcoat?**

# Further work on chapter 6

1 (a) What do you understand by the words 'fully automatic' in describing a washing machine?
(b) Name one advantage and one disadvantage in owning a fully automatic washing machine.
(c) What agents would you use to remove the following stains:
(i) blood from a cotton pillowcase; (ii) grass from white crimplene trousers; (iii) biro from a white cotton blouse?
(d) What information would you expect to get from the care label on a garment?
(e) State how you would hand wash, dry and finish a knitted woollen garment. (ALSEB)

2 (a) Many people use launderettes. Suggest two advantages and two disadvantages in making use of such facilities.
(b) 'Comfort', 'Softlan' and 'Lenor' etc. are not detergents. What is their purpose in laundry work and how are they used?
(c) What is meant by a 'synthetic' detergent?
(d) List four important points to consider when sorting the family wash.
(e) What precautions would you take when laundering a new pair of denim jeans?
(f) Suggest two important points about the care of your washing machine if it is to continue to give good results. (ALSEB)

3 Choose three models of either automatic or twin-tub washing machines now on sale. Describe each one and compare them for performance, size of wash-load, value for money, cost to run and any other factors. Use 'Which?' magazine to help you.

4 (a) At what stage during washing would you use a fabric softener?
(b) Give two rules to prevent creasing non-iron fabrics during laundering.
(c) What will happen if a white nylon article is dried in strong sunlight?
(d) Underline the fabric in the following list which may be safely boiled
– wool, terylene, white linen, red cotton, nylon. (EMREB)

5 Make a study of the development of methods of washing and ironing clothes, from early times through to the invention of the first washing machines and up to the present day.

**Books for further reading**

*Science and your Home* **J Gostelow** Blond Educational
*Simple Laundrywork and Fabric Care* **M I Mennie** Mills and Boon
*Fabrics and Laundrywork* **Gawthorpe** Hulton Educational
Procter and Gamble – Educational Literature
Lever Brothers Ltd – Educational Literature

# Chapter 7
# Managing your money

# Budgeting and saving

## Budgeting

Everyone has to plan carefully if they are to make the best possible use of their money. First of all you have to decide on the most important expenses, e.g.:

Rent or mortgage
Rates – *council*
Food
Gas, electricity, other fuel – *petrol*
Clothing

When you have done this, you can use the rest of your money to cover other needs, such as:

Fares
Pets
Garden
Holidays
Entertainment
Newspapers
Insurances
Saving

1 Imagine your family consists of husband, wife and two small children. List all the expenses you might have, as in this diagram.

| | |
|---|---|
| Rent or mortgage (about 20%)<br>Rates<br>Food (about 25%)<br>Fuel (about 10%)<br>Clothing (about 15%)<br>Fares<br>Entertainment<br>Newspapers<br>Holidays<br>Gardening<br>Pets<br>Insurances<br>Savings | |
| Total £ | |

2 Then give yourself a certain amount of money per week and put it down as the total.
3 Divide this total among your expenses, so that it adds up.
4 Some bills, like gas and electricity, are only paid one a quarter. You will have to work out how much to allow each week for them.
5 Other bills, such as the mortgage, are paid only once a month. Again, you will have to work out how much to allow for this.

## Saving

It is a good idea to try to save some money for a special item you want, or for unexpected expenses. There are various ways of doing this.

1 *In a piggy-bank* at home. You can also buy special money boxes with different compartments for gas, coal, rent or similar expenses.

2 *The Post Office.* Anyone over 7 can open a savings account. You can deposit any sum between 25p and £10 000. You can withdraw up to £20 on demand. You are paid interest (about 4%) on your money.

3 *Trustee Savings Bank.* This works in a similar way to the Post Office, but you can withdraw larger sums of money. They will also arrange to pay your bills for you.

4 *Building Societies.* This is a good way of saving if you want to buy a house, as the Building Societies are more likely to lend you money if you have saved with them regularly. You are paid interest (about 10%) on your money.

5 *Premium bonds* are bought in £5 units. You are not paid interest but you have the chance of winning a money prize, between £50 and £250 000, from thousands of prizes drawn every week.

6 *Save As You Earn,* 'S.A.Y.E.'. You can arrange to have money taken from your wages before you receive them. This is for regular saving.

7 *Bank accounts,* for example at the Midland, Barclays, Lloyds or National Westminster Banks. They have two sorts of accounts, current and deposit (see page 141). A deposit account is better for saving as you receive interest on your money.

---

### Questions

1 **You want to save £80 to spend on a holiday. How would you save this money? Why?**
2 **You are saving to get married in two years' time. What method would you choose, and why?**
3 **You want to save for a new winter coat. How would you do it?**
4 **Find out the current rate of interest paid by**
a **a Post Office savings account**
b **a Building Society account.**

# Insurance

Insurances help to provide you with financial security in case of unexpected events or losses. The principle behind all insurance is that you make regular payments to an insurance company as a safeguard against certain events happening to you, such as fire, theft, or a car accident. If this event should happen, then the insurance company will pay you a previously agreed amount of money to help compensate you for the loss or damage.

There are many insurance companies in business. You will find them in any high street or shopping centre. They offer many different kinds of insurance.

## Life insurance

It is a very good idea for the breadwinner of the family to take out a life insurance policy. This will ensure that the family is provided for if he or she should die. They can arrange for their mortgage, if they have one, to be paid off completely if any accident should happen, so that the family will still have a home.

## House insurance

### Buildings

If you borrow money to buy a house, the Building Society (or whoever gives you the mortgage) will insist that you insure the house against fire or other damage so that their property is protected.

As house prices usually increase, you must review the amount you have the house insured for every year.

### Contents

It is in your own interest to insure the contents of your house – furniture, carpets, television, cooker, clothing, and so on – against accidents such as fire, theft or flood. The premium you pay depends on the value of your belongings. You pay so much for every £100 worth of goods. Large or expensive items, such as jewellery or furs, should be insured separately.

There are basically two ways of insuring the contents of your house:

1   You insure the contents for their current value. If you make a claim, the insurance company will not give you the price you paid for an article when it was new, but will reduce this to the amount they consider it was worth when it was damaged or stolen, perhaps after several years' wear and tear. This means that you would be very unlikely to receive enough money to buy a new item to replace the one destroyed.

2   You can insure your household goods so that you receive the full amount it would cost you to replace them. The premium for this kind of insurance will be higher.

No insurance can really make up for your house being burgled, so take precautions. When you leave your house, make sure that the doors are locked and windows secured. When going on holiday, remember to cancel milk and newspapers.

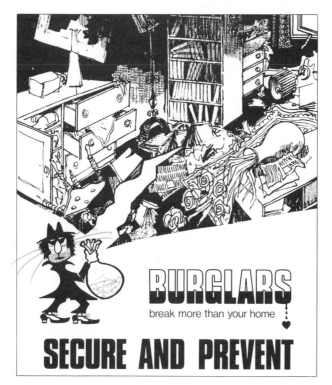

BURGLARS

break more than your home

SECURE AND PREVENT

**Holiday insurance**

You can insure against any possible risks you take when going on holiday. These could include:

1 Cover of medical expenses if you are taken ill or have an accident while you are abroad, where treatment has to be paid for.
2 Loss of money, tickets or luggage.
3 Cancellation of a holiday, for example if you are taken ill and can't go, but still have to pay the hotel bill.
4 Extra hotel or travelling expenses which you might have on your journey, for example if you can't travel to your destination as planned because public transport services are not working normally due to industrial action such as strikes or 'go-slows'.

---

Questions

1 **What is the general purpose of all insurance?**
2 **Why should a young couple take out a life insurance policy if they decide to buy a home?**
3 **Why does a Building Society insist that you insure your house when they lend you money to buy it?**
4 **Think about your living-room at home. Work out how much it would cost to replace everything in it, new. Do the same for the rest of your home.**
5 **Describe the risks you should insure against when going on holiday abroad.**

# Advertising

You are protected against untrue or misleading advertisements by the Trade Descriptions Act of 1968, which makes it illegal for any advertisement, label or spoken statement to mislead people.

But you must protect yourself against adverts which try to persuade you that you need certain goods.

Advertising is big business. Many firms spend a great deal of money employing advertising companies to think up advertisements for their products, to persuade you to part with your money to buy their goods.

Everywhere we go we see advertisements tempting us to spend money. They are on television and radio, at the cinema, on posters, in magazines, and on leaflets pushed through our letter boxes.

Clever advertising tries to make you think you could be happier, more important, a better mother, or more attractive, if you use particular products.

The advertisers know that this is how you would like to feel.

They are trying to sell feelings. They want you to think that you will become like the person in the advert if you use their products: happy, popular, well-to-do and good looking.

But do you really think it is true? Is it as easy as that? If you use a certain brand of shampoo, will you have lots more boyfriends than you have now? If a housewife buys a certain brand of baked beans will she really become the good-humoured, well-dressed mother in the immaculate modern kitchen of the television advertisements? Or if a man uses a particular kind of after-shave lotion can he really expect to be like the man in the advert, with an expensive sports car and a stream of attractive girls following him everywhere?

The products may be good – the people who make them will probably go to a lot of trouble to make sure of this before spending money on advertising them. But remember, all you really get when you buy the product is a bottle of shampoo, a packet of soap powder, or a tin of beans. You don't get the life-style shown in the advertisement.

So be on your guard against clever advertising. Try to decide for yourself what you need and what is the best value for money, and spend your money as wisely as you can.

Questions

1 **Are television or magazine adverts, or any others, allowed to make false claims?**
2 **What law was passed to prevent this?**
3 **What kind of feelings do advertisers want you to associate with their goods?**
4 **Do you think that if you use a certain product, e.g. shampoo or toothpaste, it will make you feel a happier person? Why is this?**
5 **Choose two advertisements now being shown on television or in magazines. For each one say:**
a **at whom do you think it is mainly aimed (e.g. mothers, young children, young people?)**
b **why do you think it is likely to make people buy the product?**

# Hire-purchase

If you buy something on credit, you take the goods and pay for them later. You usually pay <u>more</u> for goods bought on credit than for the same goods bought for cash, because you have to pay interest.

The advantage of buying this way is that you do not have to pay the whole cost at once, but can spread it over a longer period.

Hire-purchase (H.P.) is one way of buying on credit. It can be useful for large, essential items that would take a long time to save for, such as furniture or a car. It is better to use hire-purchase only to buy goods you need, not those you would just like to have. You must be careful not to buy so much on H.P. that your weekly payments become difficult to keep up.

Remember these important points when you buy anything on hire-purchase:

1  The goods do not belong to you until you have made the very last payment.

2  If you have paid more than one-third of the price, and you fall behind with the payments, the dealer cannot take them away from you without a court order. You will still have to pay for them, but the court will decide how much you have to pay, and how often.

3  If a salesman comes to your home and you sign an agreement there, the law allows you three days to change your mind after signing. This is because the law recognizes that you are more likely to be talked into buying goods you don't really need when you are in your own home rather than in a shop.
   If you have paid a deposit, you are entitled to have it returned to you.

4   You will pay more for goods bought on credit. If, for example, you buy a gas cooker which costs £200 cash, you may have to pay about £228 to buy it on hire-purchase, because you have to pay interest charges. The rate of interest varies between one shop and another, so shop around for the best rate. Large stores and electricity boards often charge lower rates of interest than small shops. When you go to buy the item, the shop must tell you the cash price and the total hire-purchase price so that you will realize how much extra it will cost you to buy it on hire-purchase.

£200 cash    12 Monthly PAYMENTS OF £19

5   If you have any complaints about goods bought on H.P., you must take them up with the finance company you have the H.P. agreement with, not the shop where you bought the goods as is normally the case.

6   If you read the hire-purchase agreement and find it difficult to understand, or find it difficult to keep up payments, you can get free advice from the Citizens' Advice Bureau. This exists to help people with any problems like this – legal, financial or about consumer affairs. They are there to help all citizens, free of charge. Their address is always in the phone book.

Questions

1   **What are (a) the advantages, and (b) the disadvantages of buying on credit?**
2   **Why shouldn't you buy too much on hire-purchase?**
3   **Why do you pay more for goods bought on hire-purchase?**
4   **You are thinking of buying a washing machine on hire-purchase. What are the most important points to remember?**
5   **How can you get help in understanding hire-purchase agreements?**
6   **How would you find the Citizens' Advice Bureau in your area?**

# Buying on credit

### Mail order

This is quite a popular way of buying goods on credit. An agent keep a catalogue and you choose your goods from it. A wide variety of goods are offered: clothing, household goods, sporting equipment, jewellery, toys, etc.

The agent orders the goods for you and if you decide to keep them you pay the agent a certain amount each week until they are paid for. If for any reason you don't want to keep the goods, the agent will send them back post free.

The agent receives about 10% commission on all the goods she sell For example, if she sells goods worth £100 she may be allowed £10 of good free for herself.

Mail-order buying is useful because you can spread the cost over several weeks – you don't have to pay the full cost at once. But you can ofte buy the goods cheaper in the shops for cash, so it may be more expensive in the end.

### Budget accounts

Customers in many large stores now open Budget Accounts (sometimes also called Continuous Credit Accounts).

You agree to pay the store a certain sum each month, for example £ Then you are allowed to have goods worth a certain amount, for example £6 In two months you will have paid off £12 of what you owe. Then you can ha another £12 worth of goods, still only paying £6 a month. Usually you pay the store a small charge for this service.

### Credit cards

Examples of these are the Access card and Barclaycard. (You don't have to have a Barclays' bank account to have a Barclaycard.)

You apply to the bank for a card and they agree to allow you a certain credit limit.

You can use the card to pay bills in shops, garages, and hotels, and to pay train and air fares. You can also use it abroad, wherever you see the signs displayed.

Instead of paying the bills in cash you give them your card to check, and you sign for the goods. Later in the month, Barclaycard or Access send you a statement, telling you how much you owe them. Then you pay them, either at once, or you can spread the repayments over a convenient period. In the latter case they charge you for this service.

### Questions

1 **Why do you think mail order buying is popular?**
2 **List the disadvantages of buying goods by mail order.**
3 **Why do you think stores encourage their customers to open Budget Accounts?**
4 **List the kind of places where you can use a credit card.**
5 **You buy some petrol using your credit card. When you actually pay for it later, to whom do you send the money?**

# Consumer protection

There are many laws and organizations which exist to protect the rights and interests of consumers or shoppers.

You ought to know <u>your</u> legal rights when you go shopping so that you can make sure you always get good value for your money.

Here are just two of the many laws which have been passed to mak sure that everyone can get a fair deal when they are shopping.

### The Sale of Goods Act, 1893

This says that:

a   All goods must be fit to be sold, that is, they must be of good enough quality to work properly. For example, clothes must not come apart when you wear them. Electrical goods must work.

b   They must be suitable for the purpose for which you buy them. Discuss with the shopkeeper the use you are going to make of the goods, then it is his responsibility to sell you only something suitable.

c   All goods must be as they are labelled or described.

So if you buy a pair of shoes and they come apart at the seams after week's wear, you should take them back to the shop.

The shop must either change them or refund your money. It is the responsibility of the shopkeeper to do this, not the manufacturer of the good He must keep the law, so politely insist on your legal rights.

### The Trade Descriptions Act 1968

This makes it illegal for any <u>labels</u>, <u>advertisements</u> or <u>spoken statements</u> to mislead customers.

For example, if you book a holiday in a caravan 'with beautiful views the sea, only one minute from the beach', then this must actually be true.

*Sale bargains*

If you buy an article at the sales which says it is 'reduced from £10 to £4', it must really have been on sale for £10 for at least 28 days out of the last six months.

## Guarantees

Sometimes in the past, if you signed a guarantee, you signed away your legal rights without realizing it.

But now there is a law which prevents manufacturers of goods from getting out of their obligations, that is, to provide you with goods that are:

a   fit for sale.
b   fit for the purpose they are sold for.
c   just as they have been advertised.

Now, no guarantee can take away your legal rights. Sometimes it adds to your normal rights, so it is worth signing. Often it is the quickest way of getting any faulty new equipment put right.

## Bar coding

Many of the products we buy from supermarkets or large stores have a square of numbered black lines of varying thickness on the wrapping. The square is a 'bar code' and is part of an electronic system increasingly being used in shops.

Each line of the 13-bar code gives certain information. The first two reveal the country the product has come from, the next five reveal the manufacturer of the product, the next five identify the product itself. The thirteenth line is an accuracy check.

As you take your purchases out of your basket at the checkout the assistant will pass the code on each product through a laser scan. The laser unit is linked to a computer which holds the price of each item. The price is retrieved from the computer file, displayed on the till for the customer to see, and both the name of the product and its price are printed on the receipt. This means that it is easy to check exactly what you have bought and what it has cost, when you get home. At the same time the computer records the sale of each item so that the shop knows at any time how much of any product has been sold and how much is in stock.

---

Questions

1   **Why do you think everyone should know their legal rights when they are shopping?**
2   **What are the three main provisions of the Sale of Goods Act?**
3   **If you bought a new coat, and the stitching came undone the first time you wore it, what would you do?**
4   **How is the Trade Descriptions Act useful?**
5   **If you bought a new washing machine would you bother to sign and send off the guarantee that came with it? Why?**
6   **What is a 'bar code'? How is it useful to (a) the customer and (b) the shop?**

# Consumer advice

## The Consumers' Association

This is an independent association formed to give information and advice to consumers.

It publishes a magazine called 'Which?' You can take out a regular subscription to this, or look at it in your local library.

250 **Refrigerators without frozen food compartments** (smallest first)

| KEY TO RATINGS | Philips ARB169 £95 Italy | Hotpoint 21160 £90 UK | Bosch KS182TRW £155 W Germany | DKK H185 £60 E Germany |
|---|---|---|---|---|
| ■ best ◢ □ ◪ ■ worst | | | | *good value* |
| Similar models | | 22160 £80 (has frozen food compartment) | KS183ERW £201 list, (built-in) KS172TLW £231 list (has frozen food compartment) | |
| Matching freezer | AFB063 £109 | 27120 £109 | GS144W £245 list | |
| Dimensions h x w x d | 85 x 55 x 60cm | 85 x 55 x 60cm | 85 x 60 x 60cm | 106 x 55 x 59cm |
| depth with door open | 113cm | 113cm | 117cm | 111cm |
| width for full access | 58cm | 94cm (now modified to 57cm) | 88cm | 59cm |
| door reversible? | yes | no | yes | no |
| Usable capacity | 149 litres 3 standard loads | 150 litres 3 standard loads | 164 litres almost 4 standard loads | 171 litres almost 4 standard loads |
| Performance temperature control | ■ | ◢ | ◢ | □ |
| quarterly running cost | □ £1.75 (58kWh) | □ £1.90 (63kWh) | ◢ £1.30 (44kWh) | □ £2.15 (72kWh) |
| Convenience | ◢ shelves not adjustable but could be pulled forward without tipping; a lot of space for bottles; bottle flap; 6-egg rack not easy to use (flap hinges upwards); plastic shelf over deep crisper bent when loaded, making opening crisper difficult; worktop | ◢ shelves not adjustable; poor door handle; rack for 9 eggs; drink dispenser (removable); laminated worktop | □ good range of shelf adjustment; half of one shelf removable to allow for large items; large crispers, but bottom ridge made them difficult to use; good 18-egg rack but lid to dairy section hinges upward (awkward); worktop | ◢ only one extra position for shelves (adjustment difficult) but adjustable door racks; space for 17 eggs; lid to dairy section a bit stiff; bottle flap; some sharpish edges |
| defrosting | ■ automatic | ■ automatic | ■ automatic | ■ automatic |
| Noise | □ | □ | ◢ | ◢ |
| Electrical safety | BEAB approved | BEAB approved | satisfactory | satisfactory |
| Which? Verdict | Good performance but not very convenient. Rather expensive for its size | Fairly good performance but not very convenient. Rather expensive for its size | Good performance, but very expensive for its size | Fair performance. Generally convenient but ours was noisy. Very cheap |

The purpose of 'Which?' is to provide useful information about a very wide range of goods, to help you always to get the best possible value for money.

Representatives of the Consumers' Association go shopping in the normal way and buy and test all kinds of goods, from cars to cosmetics, from sausages to washing up liquid, from grocery prices to washing machines.

They carefully test all the goods they buy to see if they are:
safe
good value for money
well made
durable
easy to service
reliable.

They tell you what to look out for when you buy certain items. Often they will recommend a 'best-buy'. They can save you from making expensive mistakes.

## The Citizens' Advice Bureau

The Citizens' Advice Bureau provides a very useful service. The service is run and paid for by local authorities, often with unpaid voluntary helpers. They will advise you, free of charge and in confidence, on almost any matter.

If you have problems as a consumer — for example, if you have difficulty with shops who refuse to replace shoddy goods and you feel you have not been fairly treated, you can go to your Citizens' Advice Bureau for advice.

Here are just a few of the many problems they can help you with:

Consumer affairs, your rights as a shopper
Legal problems, about insurance, pensions, Social Security, taxation
Personal matters, wills, marriage, divorce, housing, neighbours
Information about places and events
Jobs, training, evening classes

They have offices in most large towns and cities. You can find their address in the local phone book.

---

Questions

1 **What is the name of the magazine published by the Consumers' Association?**
2 **What is the purpose of the magazine?**
3 **You are thinking about buying a new cooker, but are confused by all the different models that are for sale. Where can you find information about the good and bad points of each?**
4 **If you were thinking of buying a washing machine, what are some of the points you would want to know about it?**
5 **Does the Citizens' Advice Bureau charge you for their advice?**
6 **If a shopkeeper refused to replace a pair of shoes which split the first time you wore them, what could you do?**

# Labelling schemes

You will often find labels attached to goods when you go shopping. Many of these labels are a sign of quality and reliability. They will only be attached to goods which have passed careful tests for safety and quality.

You will find these labels attached to a variety of goods, including gas and electrical appliances. When you see them, you will know that the goods are worth buying.

Here are some of the labels you should look out for.

The B.S.I. (British Standards Institution) tests a wide variety of goods sent to them by manufacturers. They carry out strict tests on the goods for quality, durability and safety. Only those products which meet the high standards of the B.S.I. are allowed to have the Kitemark attached to them.

This means that when you see any article in the shops which displays the Kitemark you can be confident that it will be a well-made product of reliable quality. Many different products carry the Kitemark, including babies' cots, crash helmets, paint, car windscreens and seat belts.

Either or both of these labels may be attached to gas appliances such as cookers and gas fires as a mark of safety and quality.

The B.E.A.B. (British Electrotechnical Approvals Board) also has its own safety mark attached to or engraved on electrical appliances, including cookers, hairdriers and irons.

Pure New Wool is a high quality material which is often imitated. When you see this label attached to garments or fabrics you can be certain that it really is wool that is:

*Pure* – not mixed with any other fibre.
*New* – not wool that has been used before and recycled.

Pure new wool

Oil heaters have caused many fires. The only safe kind to buy are those which are marked with this sign. This means that the heater

a  has a reliable guard
b  cannot be knocked over easily and
c  has a device to ensure that the flame will go out if it should accidentally be knocked over.

The Design Council has a permanent exhibition of well-designed British-made goods. If an article is 'well designed' it means that it is well made from good quality material, suitable for the purpose it is meant for and pleasing in appearance.

Goods selected by the Design Centre can display this mark as a sign of good design and quality. You may see it attached to furniture, cutlery and tableware, toys and many other household goods.

selected for the
DESIGN
CENTRE
LONDON

---

Questions

1  **When you go shopping, what is the point of looking for labels attached to goods?**
2  **Draw the labels you would expect to find attached to the following:**
a  **an electric sewing machine or power drill**
b  **a gas central heating boiler**
c  **a coffee table**
d  **a winter skirt or jumper**
e  **a portable oil heater.**
   **Beside each label write down what it would tell you about the article it was attached to.**

# Bank accounts

### Who can have a bank account?

Many people now find it useful to open a bank account when they start work. They can have their wages or salary paid to them by cheque. It is not difficult to understand how it works. If you want to open a bank account, you simply go into any branch of the banks named below, and they will arrange it for you.

### Which bank?

There are four main banks in this country. They are:
Midland
Lloyds
Barclays
National Westminster

### How does it work?

*To pay money in* you fill in a slip, and hand it over the counter with the money.

You can have your wages or salary paid straight into your account by your employer if you want to. Then he only gives you your payslip telling you how much you have earned.

*To take money out.* You are given your own cheque book to keep. If you want cash you just go to the bank and write out a cheque to yourself.

If you want to pay a bill, or buy something from a shop, you write out a cheque. You pay with this instead of with cash. Most shops insist on seeing your cheque card as a means of identification. This card is a guarantee from the bank that they will pay the shop the amount you owe them, even if you have no money in your bank account to cover it.

The bank will only give you a cheque card if you have shown yourself to be a reliable person and have kept your account in credit – which means that you don't keep writing out cheques when you have no money in your bank account.

Imagine you are out shopping. You see a coat you want to buy in a shop called J. Smith. It costs £20. If you want to pay for it by cheque, this is how you fill in one of your cheques before you give it to the shop in exchange for the coat. You keep the counterfoil as a record of what you have spent.

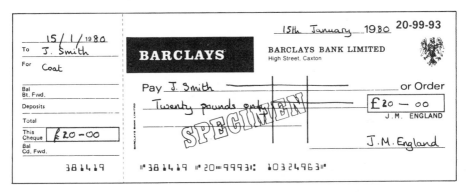

### Why have a bank account?

1 You don't need to carry large sums of money around with you, for shopping or paying bills.
2 You are less likely to be robbed if you are not carrying cash.
3 It is easy to keep a record of how much money you have.
4 Sometimes you can borrow money from the bank for large expenses, perhaps to buy a car or to modernize your home.

This kind of account, where you have a cheque book, is called a current account.

You can also have a deposit account at a bank. This is for saving money, rather than for everyday use. You earn interest on the money you have in a deposit account, but you don't have a cheque book.

### Questions

1 **You have received a bill for £18.72p from the Northern Gas Board. You want to pay by cheque. Draw a cheque correctly filled in to pay this bill.**
2 **What do you think is the most important advantage of having a current account at a bank? Why?**
3 **Would you rather be paid in cash or have your wages paid straight into your account when you start work? Explain why you feel like this.**

# Further work on chapter 7

1 Suggest the essential items to be included in the budget of a family consisting of three children and their parents.

How can good management on the part of the mother ensure the best use of the money available to her? (O)

2 (a) You are earning £40 per week net and living at home. Work out a budget showing expenditure and the weekly amount you could save for your wedding in the near future.
(b) List three popular methods of saving money.
(c) Which method would you choose and why?
(d) Explain the following terms: (i) crossed cheque; (ii) standing order; (iii) bank statement. (ALSEB)

3 The rates, which are part of the expenses of a family, are part of the income of the local authority who collects it. Try to obtain a rates demand which will show you how they balance their budget.

How much money do they have, where does the income come from, and what do they spend it on?

4 Make a list of a dozen grocery items which you might buy weekly. Visit two or three local supermarkets and make a note of the price of each item. When you get home compare the total costs of your list of items in different shops. You could arrange to do this over a few weeks, with your class or group, to find out if any one shop is consistently cheaper.

'Which?' magazine (see page 136) regularly carries out similar surveys for the benefit of its readers.

5 For what must a teenager budget when she starts work?

6 Morning papers and radio programmes often give a list of foods which are cheap and in season. Make out a list of these foods and plan menus for a day or a week to make good use of these foods. (Adapted from Oxford practical exam.)

7 (a) The following symbols are found on many household items. What do they mean? (i) the Kitemark; (ii) the Design Centre label.
(b) Giving attention to the range of goods, the prices and the service, list two advantages and two disadvantages of shopping at (i) the supermarket; (ii) the small corner shop.
(c) Having moved into a new area to live, name four points which could influence you when selecting a shop in which to do your weekly shopping.
(d) What is meant by 'date stamping' and how does it help the consumer? (ALSEB)

8   (a) Name four of the main ways of saving money.
    (b) List the main ways of buying things.
    (c) Give two advantages and two disadvantages of each of the above ways of buying.

9   The Post Office has several different saving schemes. Obtain current leaflets and outline each scheme available stating under what circumstances each would be a suitable method of saving.

10  It is very necessary for a young married couple to plan ahead to ensure successful management of their joint wage packets.
    (a) Give four items which a young married couple must include when budgeting their joint wage packets.
    (b) What value do you attach to each of the following: (i) mail-order facilities; (ii) a written guarantee; (iii) trading stamps; (iv) having a cheque book and bankers' card?
    (c) If you decide to buy some furniture on hire-purchase, what important points should you consider?
    (d) Write fully on ways in which a family can economize in these more difficult days.

11  The pressure of advertisements makes hire-purchase seem attractive. Discuss the following:
    (a) The advantages and disadvantages of hire-purchase.
    (b) When you would use this form of purchasing power.
    (c) The effect of advertising upon your choice of goods.
    (d) The ways in which money is spent upon advertising. (EAEB)

12  Is advertising of value to the housewife?
    (a) Name four different ways in which advertisements are presented.
    (b) Name one safety point to look for when buying (i) a toddler's nightdress; (ii) a painted wooden toy for a child.
    (c) Give four points to be considered when spending money on special bargain offers of food.
    (d) Draw and explain the 'Kitemark'.
    (e) What other labels are used to help the public when shopping?
    (SEREB)

13  Write fully on each of the following:
    (a) The Kitemark.
    (b) The advantages of having a bank account.
    (c) Premium Savings Bonds.
    (d) Why all insurance is a good thing. (EMREB)

14  It is important to shop wisely.
    (a) (i) What is the function of a manufacturer's guarantee?
    (ii) Why is it important to read it carefully before signing it?
    (b) What do you understand by the term Consumer Association?
    (c) What are the advantages and disadvantages of credit cards?
    (d) List the sources which are available for consumer advice. (EAEB)

15 Find out the cost of insuring the contents of your house. It usually costs so much for each £100 of goods. Enquire whether there are different prices for:
(a) insuring the goods for the amount it would cost to replace them.
(b) insuring them for their cost less an amount for the wear and tear they have received since they were bought.

16 **Consumer rights**
(a) You have bought a trouser suit by mail order which is not satisfactory. Write a letter stating exactly what is wrong.
(b) Name one group or association from which you could ask advice on your rights as a consumer if you did not get satisfaction.
(c) What advice would you give to someone who is considering buying an expensive piece of equipment?
(d) What are the advantages of having a banking account?
(e) How would you set about opening a banking account? (SEREB)

17 (a) What steps could a consumer take in the following situations:
(i) the heel breaks on a recently purchased pair of shoes; (ii) a sewing machine purchased in a store is found to be £5 cheaper in a shop in another part of town?
(b) Explain three methods used by television advertisers to persuade teenagers to buy goods.
(c) Explain Hire Purchase as a method of payment.
(d) Name two other ways of purchasing goods by a 'Buy now, pay later' method. (SCE)

18 Make a study of the facilities available in your area to help and advise the consumer. Find out from your rate demand what proportion of the rates is spent on consumer protection.

**Books for further reading**

*Home Management and House Care* **Emily Carpenter** Heinemann Educatio
*Running a Home is Fun* **Good Housekeeping Institute** Ebury Press
*Homecraft* **Margaret Clark** Routledge and Kegan Paul
*Teach Yourself Budgeting and Home Management*
**Good Housekeeping Institute** English Universities Press
*'Which?' magazine* Consumers' Association
Leaflets from the Office of Fair Trading

Chapter 8
# Looking after the family

# The expectant mother

### Diet

An unborn baby relies completely upon his mother to supply the foods he needs. He will take from her the nutrients he needs for his own body to develop and grow soundly, so she should have some knowledge of which foods are needed for this.

The mother does not need to 'eat for two' in the sense of eating twice the quantity but she does need extra foods rich in the nutrients needed for her baby to develop well and to keep herself in good health.

#### Extra foods

*Protein*. A good intake of protein foods is needed. The baby's bones, muscles, tissues and so on all contain protein. If they are to grow and develop fully he needs a good supply of protein which he can only get from his mother. An extra pint of milk daily will meet her extra need, or an increased intake of meat, cheese, fish, yoghurt, nuts or other protein-rich foods.

*Calcium* is the essential part of both the bones and teeth. If the baby is to have a strong, well-formed bone structure, then a good supply of calcium is essential. A daily pint of milk, and cheese, will provide what is needed.

*Vitamin D* (Cholecalciferol) is sometimes called the calcifying vitamin, because it is needed before the body can actually make use of calcium for the bone structure. It is found in butter, margarine, and oily fish, and is also produced by the action of sunlight on the skin.

*Vitamin C* (Ascorbic acid) is needed for the baby's normal growth, for protection against infection and to help the body absorb iron. You need a good supply of this each day, as the body does not store it. It is found in raw fruit and vegetables and in special fruit drinks (blackcurrant, rose-hip or orange), labelled as having a high Vitamin C content. Ordinary fruit squashes normally contain very little.

*Iron* is very important during pregnancy for the production of sound red blood cells. For the first three or four months of his life the baby is fed only on milk which contains very little iron. He is born with a store of iron in his liver which lasts him during this time. He will take the iron he needs from his mother before he is born. If she does not have enough iron for the needs of the baby and herself she may become anaemic, tire easily, and be weak and breathless. Plenty of iron-rich foods will avoid this — liver, kidney, red meats, corned beef, egg, egg yolk, black pudding, dried fruit, black treacle and cocoa.

The other vitamins and minerals too are important for the proper growth and development of your child. There will normally be an adequate supply of these from a good, varied diet. Try to include the following foods in your diet:

1–1½ pints of milk daily
Liver weekly
Oily fish weekly
Meat, cheese, eggs, yoghurt
Fresh fruit and vegetables
Cereals and wholegrain bread

*Foods to avoid*

Too many rich, fried, fatty or sugary foods are not good for anyone. They can make you put on too much weight and may aggravate any sickness, indigestion or heartburn you may have. Strong tea or coffee sometimes has the same effect, as does highly spiced or seasoned food.

*Smoking* can do positive damage to your baby's health. It is well worth trying to stop or cut down and to avoid places with a very smoky atmosphere.

*Alcohol* should only be drunk in moderation. Remember that alcohol is a drug and can affect your baby. It is better to avoid spirits like whisky and gin altogether.

*Extra vitamin or iron tablets* may be prescribed for you by your doctor, but you should not take them or any other medicines or tablets such as aspirins, sickness pills or laxatives without first asking medical advice, as they could affect the developing baby.

## Dental care during pregnancy

The baby will draw the calcium for forming his own bones and teeth from his mother, so you need a good supply. You should:

a   Eat plenty of foods rich in calcium – milk, cheese, white flour.
b   Visit your dentist often. Treatment is free for expectant mothers and until the baby is a year old.
c   Take extra care with cleaning your teeth. You should clean after breakfast, then after every meal if possible, and never go to bed without cleaning your teeth.

## Care of hair and skin

Keep your hair in an easily managed, easily washed style. It may become more or less greasy than usual. Your skin will often improve, especially if you take particular care about your diet.

## Ante-natal care

If you miss one period you may wonder whether you are pregnant. If you miss two it is quite probable that you are and a visit to your doctor will confirm this. He will usually send you to a local clinic for ante-natal care.

*The ante-natal clinic* provides the following services:

1   Regular medical checks are made to make sure you keep in good health.
2   Your weight gain is checked. It should not normally be more than 24–28 lbs. altogether.
3   Advice is given on any problems you may have – perhaps about diet, hygiene, preparing for breast feeding, or arranging home help.
4   Mothercraft classes are often run by local clinics, with friendly and informal advice on how to choose your baby's clothes and nursery equipment, how to feed, bath and look after him or her.
5   Relaxation classes will teach you exercises and ways of relaxing your body which help you while the baby is being born.

6   At the clinic you will meet other expectant mothers. This gives you an
    opportunity to make friends and to discuss the interests and problems you
    may have in common.

### Post-natal care

After the birth of the baby you can go back to the same clinic for
post-natal care. Here are some of the ways in which they can give you help
and advice:

1   They will check your health and give you advice on how to regain your figure.
2   Your baby's health and weight gain will be checked.
3   Vaccination for your baby will be discussed and arranged.
4   The clinic will give help and support on any problems you may have, perhaps
    with feeding your baby or with caring for him in any way.
5   They will discuss and advise you on family planning so that you can have the
    number of children you feel you would like and can look after when you want
    them.
6   They often sell welfare foods, such as dried milk and vitamin foods.
7   Again, you meet other mothers of young babies with whom you can make
    friends.

*The midwife* is concerned with the health of the mother and the baby up to two weeks old. Whether the baby is born in hospital or at home she comes to visit you at home daily until two weeks after the birth.

*The health visitor* is concerned with the baby from the age of two weeks to five years. She is a trained nurse, midwife and health visitor and will visit you at home to advise and help with the care of the baby or with coping with everyday family problems.

*Home helps* can be arranged through your doctor or clinic, to come and help at home with all the jobs a mother normally does – cooking, shopping, cleaning, washing – until the mother is fit enough to do them herself. You pay for this service according to how much you can afford.

**Financial help**

Free or cheap milk and welfare foods are available to many expectant mothers and their young children. The clinic will advise you about this.

*Maternity Grant* is a lump sum paid either before or after the baby is born. Everyone is entitled to it, provided either mother or father has paid at least twenty-six National Insurance contributions before the baby is born.

*Maternity Allowance* is a weekly allowance paid to those mothers who have been employed and paying full National Insurance contributions. It is paid for eleven weeks before the baby is due and seven weeks afterwards, provided the mother does not work at this time. It enables her to give up working in good time before the birth of the baby so that she can keep herself fit and rested, and it means that she does not need to return to work too soon afterwards.

*Child benefit* is a sum paid weekly, usually to the mother, for all the children in the family, including the first. It was formerly called the Family Allowance. An extra allowance is paid to one-parent families.

*Unmarried mothers* are entitled to the same help and benefits. They often need extra help and support, and their doctor or clinic will always put them in touch with an organization sympathetic and willing to help.

*'Lifeline'* is just one of the voluntary bodies who give free and practical help of many kinds, including help with housing, work and possible adoption, to anyone facing an unwanted pregnancy, whether married or not.

---

Questions

1 **Which nutrients should an expectant mother take extra care to include in her diet?**
2 **Name three foods which will give a good supply of each one of these.**
3 **Name some foods it may be better to avoid during pregnancy.**
4 **Is it a good idea for an expectant mother to smoke and drink a lot? Why?**
5 **How would you take particular care of your teeth during pregnancy?**
6 **How can (a) ante-natal and (b) post-natal clinics help a mother and baby?**
7 **Describe the financial help an expectant mother could expect to receive.**

# Baby care

Caring for her first baby can be a very enjoyable time for a new mother, but at the same time she may often feel anxious about many aspects of looking after him or her and may wonder whether she is doing the 'right' thing. In this country a mother can find help and advice easily, not only from her family and friends but from her doctor, midwife, clinic or health visitor.

## Feeding

### Breast-feeding
Whenever possible, a baby should be breast-fed, because:

1   Breast milk contains exactly what is required for the baby's needs.
2   It is always clean, fresh and at the right temperature.
3   It contains substances which help the baby resist infection.
4   It costs nothing and is readily available.
5   It takes no time to prepare feeds or sterilize bottles.
6   It helps the development of a close and affectionate relationship between mother and baby.

### Bottle-feeding
This may sometimes be necessary, in which case the baby is fed on cow's milk, either dried, fresh or evaporated. It is extremely important to follow exactly the advice of your doctor or clinic about the quantities the baby needs, and the correct preparation of feeds.

Bottle-feeding does have these advantages:

1   It means a baby can be fed even if his mother cannot feed him.
2   Someone else can feed the baby if the mother is not available.
3   You can see exactly how much milk the child is getting.

A bottle-fed baby should always be held closely and affectionately by his mother, so that he feels as secure and loved as a breast-fed baby would

*Cleanliness*

Everything concerned with a baby's milk must be absolutely clean. Harmful bacteria will quickly grow in milk and could cause serious illness. Your hands and everything you use should be well washed before you prepare a bottle. Bottles and teats must be sterilized after use.

*Sterilizing bottles*

This can be done by (a) rinsing, washing, then boiling bottles and teats for the correct length of time, or (b) rinsing, washing, then soaking bottles and teats in a special hypochlorite solution (the 'Milton' method). Whichever method you use it is essential to get exact instructions from your clinic and to follow them exactly.

**Extra vitamin-rich foods**

Your clinic or doctor will advise you as to exactly when and how to introduce these foods to give your baby the best possible start. From the age of a few weeks, he may need extra nutrients which are lacking in breast milk and cow's milk.

*Vitamin C* can be provided by special fruit juice or syrup, usually orange or rose-hip.
*Vitamins A and D* are usually supplied by drops of a cod-liver oil preparation.
*Iron* can be provided by sieved egg yolk.

These vitamins, foods and also dried milk are usually sold at your local clinic.

**Weaning**

This means introducing solid foods to a baby who has only been used to milk. Weaning is a gradual process during which you should aim to get him or her used to a varied diet, beginning with finely mashed or sieved foods. He may not like the feeling of a spoon and food in his mouth at first as he has only been used to sucking, so it is best to give him just a little solid food to taste at the beginning of a feed when he is still hungry enough to try it.

---

Questions

1 **Suggest five ways in which a mother could find help or advice if she had any problems in caring for her small child.**
2 **What do you think are the four most important reasons for breast-feeding a baby?**
3 **Why do you think some mothers do not breast-feed their babies?**
4 **Why is extra care about cleanliness needed when preparing babies' bottles?**
5 **Briefly describe two possible ways of sterilizing bottles and teats. Which method would you advise a mother to use and why?**
6 **What are the reasons why babies should never be left alone to feed themselves from a bottle?**
7 **Name four nutrients needed by a growing baby which milk does not supply. Say how you would provide your baby with each one.**
8 **Describe how you would start to wean your baby on to solid food.**

# Clothes for a baby

Clothes for a young baby should be soft, warm and light, made of absorbent material, easy to put on and take off and easy to wash and iron. Do not be tempted to buy too many of the first size as the baby will very quickly grow out of them.

### The layette

A layette means the clothes you collect in preparation for an expected baby. It will include most of the articles listed below, and will depend partly on the time of year the baby is born.

*Nappies* – at least two dozen.

*Vests.* These should be either pure wool or cotton, depending on the time of year. They should be easy to put on and take off without pulling. Either an 'envelope-style' neck or a front-opening type fastened with ribbon is best.

*Stretch-towelling suits* are ideal for wear during the day or night. They cover the baby from below his head to his toes and leave no gaps. They can be easily machine-washed and do not need ironing. They stretch a little as the baby grows and so last quite well, though of course they should not be allowed to become too tight.

*Nightgowns* may be worn instead of stretch suits. They are often made of winceyette (brushed cotton) which is a highly inflammable material. This means they are only suitable for a small baby who is too young to crawl around. (See page 157.)

*Matinee jackets* are light, knitted cardigans, used for extra warmth whenever needed.

*Hats, bootees and mittens* for cooler weather. You can also buy smooth mittens which help to stop babies scratching their faces.

*Shawl or soft blanket.* A small baby likes to be firmly wrapped up at first. A knitted or cellular small blanket or shawl is ideal.

*Bibs*, usually made of towelling, protect a baby's clothes during a feed. They may be plastic-backed, and for safety must be taken off after the feed.

### Nappies

There are many different types of nappies available. By trying different kinds a mother can find out what suits her and her baby best.

1  *Towelling nappies* are soft and absorbent. You will need a couple of dozen at least.

2  *Muslin nappies* are thinner and lighter. They may be used instead of towelling nappies for a very small baby or in hot weather.

3  *Disposable nappies*, worn inside plastic pants, are thick and soft. They save you having to wash nappies but it can be rather expensive to use them all the time. It is better to burn them than to flush them away, as they are quite a frequent cause of blocked drains.

4   *Nappy liners* are like strong paper handkerchiefs worn inside a towelling nappy. They will hold any soiling and can be flushed away easily so that the outer nappy is easier to wash.

5   *One-way nappies*, made of soft material, are worn inside a towelling nappy. The moisture passes through to the outer nappy and the side next to the baby's skin stays dry, cutting down the risk of nappy rash.

### Washing

Babies' skin is particularly sensitive, so only a mild detergent should be used for their clothes. Rinsing should be thorough. The use of a fabric conditioner will keep the clothes soft.

Nappies should be soaked and washed in very hot water or boiled. This will keep them white and kill any germs which could cause nappy rash. Rinse them well and dry them out of doors or in a tumble-drier to keep them soft.

Instead of washing, nappies may be soaked in a solution of sanitizing powder. This will whiten them and kill any bacteria. Rinse them well in cold water afterwards and dry as usual.

### Equipment

Look for the following points when choosing equipment for your baby.

*Pram* – good brakes, waterproof mattress, will not tip easily, collapsible if you want to take it in a car, fittings for a safety harness, comfortable to push.

*Cot* – firm, waterproof mattress, lead-free paint, bars not too far apart, strongly made, a drop-side with a firm catch. Look for the Kitemark.

*Bath and stand* – make sure they are firm and steady.

*High or Low Chair* – steady, easy to clean, fitting for a safety harness.

*Nursing chair* – with low legs so the baby will not easily roll off your lap.

### Toiletries

Many toiletries are specially made for babies' delicate skins. They include baby lotion and oil for cleaning, creams to protect the skin from nappy rash, talcum powder, mild soap and shampoo, cotton wool and cotton buds.

---

Questions

1   **When choosing any clothes for a small baby, what qualities would you look for?**
2   **What clothes are included in a layette? Say what you would look for when choosing each one.**
3   **Describe the different kinds of nappies you can buy, giving the advantages and disadvantages of each kind.**
4   **What general rules would you follow when washing clothes for a baby?**
5   **You are helping a friend choose a pram, cot and baby bath and stand. What safety features would you advise her to look for, for each item?**

# The safety of children

## Vaccination

Vaccines are available to protect children from several serious infections, including poliomyelitis (polio), diphtheria, tetanus and whooping cough, all of which were once common causes of serious illness and death.

It is important for parents to know what vaccines are available for preventing disease in their children and to know both the benefits and the possible risks.

### Polio

Polio often causes permanent paralysis and in some cases death. The general use of vaccination has nearly eliminated the disease, but when this happens and parents feel it is not worth vaccinating their children, there can be a sudden increase in the number of cases of polio in unvaccinated children. Polio vaccine very seldom has any harmful effects. Only rarely – once in more than a million cases – has a person who has received the vaccine developed paralysis.

### Diphtheria/Tetanus/Whooping Cough – Triple Vaccine

Vaccination against these three diseases may be combined in one vaccine which gives protection against all three, though they can all be given separately if it should be wished.

### Diphtheria

This is a very serious infection of the nose and throat. National vaccination has reduced the number of cases from 50 000 a year to less than 10 in 1977.

### Tetanus

This results from infected wounds or cuts which may appear only slight in themselves. It is a severe disease and can kill, but it can be prevented by vaccination.

### Whooping cough

This is a highly infectious and distressing chest infection which can damage the lungs. Babies can suffer seriously from it and may die.

Following evidence that whooping cough vaccine has, in a very small number of cases, resulted in a serious reaction affecting the brain and nervous system, it has become less of a routine vaccination. The decision, of course, rests finally with the parents. Unfortunately, though, this reduced number of children receiving vaccinations has led to a sharp increase in the number of whooping-cough cases reported, from 4000 in 1976 to over 17000 in 1977.

It is important for parents to realize that when they decide which diseases to have their children vaccinated against, they should base their decision on a careful study of the facts and figures available, and they should discuss their own particular case with their doctor or health visitor. There is no doubt at all that vaccination has very effectively reduced the likelihood of a child developing a serious disease and the risk of any serious reaction from the vaccination itself is very uncommon.

Doubts about the whooping-cough vaccine should not deter parents from having the other vaccinations available to their children. A 'scare' that vaccination is likely to cause serious illness may make parents decide against vaccination, but when this happens the number of cases of the disease increases, so that unvaccinated children are then more likely to develop the infection as a result.

Your local clinic will start a suitable programme of vaccination in babyhood and this will be completed when the child goes to school. A careful record should be kept of which vaccinations were given and when, as it is easy to forget details when the programme is spread over a number of years.

## Safety rules when looking after babies

1   Do not use a pillow for young babies – it is not necessary. A firm, flat safety pillow is the only safe kind if you must use one at all.
2   Tuck babies in firmly, so that blankets cannot cover the face.
3   Put a baby to sleep on his side rather than his back, so that if he brings up a little feed he will not choke on it.
4   A baby should not sleep with adults or older children, because of the danger of smothering.
5   Do not use plastic sheets or covers in cots or prams, as this could lead to suffocation.
6   Never leave a baby alone with a plastic bib on.
7   Never leave a baby alone to suck from a bottle, as he could easily choke.
8   Use a safety net to keep cats from sleeping on the baby when he is out in his pram. The cat may be attracted by the warmth.
9   As soon as a baby can sit up make sure he is securely harnessed into his pram or high chair, which should be steady.
10  Keep small buttons, beads or toys away from a baby, as he will automatically put them in his mouth.

**The safety of young children**

Many serious accidents happen at home every year. Children under five have a particularly high number of accidents, as you can see from these figures for one particular year.

| Cause of accident | Age 0–4 years | Age 5–14 years |
|---|---|---|
| Suffocation/choking | 664 | 11 |
| Poisoning | 71 | 17 |
| Falls | 66 | 11 |

### Suffocation and choking

Suffocation and choking cause death as the child is unable to breathe. Follow all the rules given above when looking after small babies. Once babies start to walk and explore there are more dangers to avoid:

1. A few inches of water can drown a small child. Never leave him alone to play in the bath or near a shallow pool or stream.
2. Keep all polythene bags out of the reach of children.
3. An old refrigerator should have the door removed before being thrown away, as a small child could get trapped inside.
4. Cut food into small pieces. Remove bones, eggshell and 'stringy' meat and vegetables.

### Poisoning

1. Keep all pills, medicines and tablets right out of a child's reach. Remember that a determined child will climb up on chairs or tables. A cupboard with a lock is best and 'child-proof' bottle tops have proved to be much safer than ordinary ones.
2. Keep household cleaners out of the reach of the toddler. Many are highly poisonous. Bleach, disinfectant, polishes, cleansing liquids and powders, and turpentine are within easy reach of a curious child in many households, often under the sink.
3. Garden sprays, weedkillers, paints, paraffin and so on should be out of reach in a garage or shed. All of these could kill if swallowed.
4. Never put chemicals, cleaners or anything else into an empty squash or lemonade bottle. A child could drink it, thinking it was lemonade.
5. Some common garden plants are poisonous. These include rhubarb leaves, privet, laburnum seeds, holly and other berries. Teach children not to eat things picked up in the garden.
6. Town gas is poisonous. Do not leave a child alone where he could turn on a gas tap.
7. Always use lead-free paint for anything a child might chew – cots and toys especially. Lead is poisonous and can cause brain damage.

### Falls

1. Have a firm safety gate at the top and bottom of the stairs.
2. Try to avoid leaving toys around the floor.
3. Do not have highly polished floors or loose mats. Mop up spills straight away.
4. Take care with open windows and balconies. Do not leave chairs near them which children could use to climb on.
5. Do not leave small children on a table even for a few seconds.
6. A cot should have the B.S.I. Kitemark. The fastening should be strong and the sides should be high enough.

7 Loose, poorly-fitting shoes can cause a fall.

8 Prams and high chairs should be steady, with a fitting for a safety harness.

### Scalds and burns

1 Unguarded fires are dangerous and illegal. Take extra care with portable fires.

2 Keep matches away from children.

3 Do not let pan handles stick out over the edge of a cooker.

4 Avoid tablecloths hanging down over the edge of the table where they could be pulled. Keep hot tea-pots away from the edge of the table.

5 Test bath water before putting a child in.

6 Take care when drinking or carrying hot liquids such as tea or coffee.

7 Flame-proof material should be used for clothes where possible. All nighties and frilly party dresses for children must, by law, be made of flame-proof material. This should be carefully washed to keep its finish. Avoid buying winceyette (brushed cotton) for making children's nightdresses. It is highly inflammable and should never be used for this purpose.

### Road safety

Train your child from the beginning in road safety, and always set a good example yourself. Do not leave children to play in a garden where they could run on to the road.

### Child safety in cars

Under the law which came into effect in January 1983, it is the responsibility of the driver to ensure that any child under 14 in the front seat of a car wears a seat belt or restraint. Any child over the age of one can wear any approved child restraint or seat belt. A child under one must be in an approved restraint designed for a child of that age or size. All adults and children over 14 are responsible themselves for wearing a seat belt.

Although the law insists only on seat belts for the front of the car as it is the most dangerous place, responsible parents can make their child safer by fitting a child safety seat, harness, seat belt or carry cot straps.

---

### Questions

1 **Name four illnesses which can be prevented by vaccination.**

2 **What points would you as a parent consider when deciding about vaccinations for your child?**

3 **Where can you get information on the different vaccines available?**

4 **How would you usually know when your child was due for a vaccination?**

5 **Why do you think young babies are particularly likely to suffocate?**

6 **What points would you be especially careful about when putting a baby to sleep in a cot or pram?**

7 **What precautions can you take to avoid a small child suffocating or choking?**

8 **Your three-year-old cousin is coming to stay with your family for a few days. Describe the precautions you would take around the house to prevent the possibility of the child being poisoned.**

9 **Name some of the most common causes of accidental falls in the home.**

10 **What precautions can you take to avoid scalds and burns?**

# Children under school age

Children have many needs which have to be met if they are to grow into happy, healthy adults. For pre-school children, all these needs should be met either at home or in pre-school nursery groups of various kinds.

### Physical care

Physical care is the most obvious need. Children have to be properly fed and kept clean and warm. They need suitable activity to become physically well developed and healthy. A good nursery will provide well-chosen equipment in an area specially planned to suit the children.

### Emotional and social development

Children have to learn to cope with their feelings about themselves and about other people. The first feelings of a small baby will all centre on himself, then he gradually extends his feelings to his mother, then his closest family and slowly he becomes sufficiently self-confident to be able to cope with a larger group outside his own family circle. A good nursery class or group can encourage this development at a rate the child can manage, by widening the circle of adults and other children he mixes with.

A child's emotional development affects the whole of his personality. Patterns can be set up in the first few years of his life which affect both the way he gets on with other people and his ability to learn and generally manage for the rest of his life.

### Intellectual development

The first five years or so of a child's life are vital in the development of his intelligence. This is important not only to his educational future but to his ability to grow into an independent, thinking adult.

The child should be provided with a variety of stimulating activities and experiences which will encourage him to think for himself, to work things out and to explore and understand his environment. He should be encouraged to use words and language so that he can learn to organize and express his thoughts.

**Why day-care for pre-school children is needed**

Until quite recently it was accepted as normal that nearly all mothers who had children should stay at home to look after them. As long as the mother wants to do this and is able to provide a warm, affectionate and interesting family life, this is probably the best background a child can have, particularly in the first few years of his life.

However, there are many reasons why this is not always possible and the role of women is changing because of them.

1 Many women want to go out to work. They enjoy the companionship and independence this gives them. This does not mean that they do not want children but rather that they want children *and* a job, so that care for their children under school age is needed.

2 Most families are now limited in size so that by the time a woman is in her late twenties or early thirties she may have had all the children she plans to have, and so is less tied to her home.

3 Housework takes less time than it did with the widespread use of convenience foods, washing machines, vacuum cleaners, refrigerators, freezers and so on. This means women have more time to spare.

4 The cost of living – including housing, fuel, food and clothing – may be so high that a family may need the extra income from the mother's job to provide an acceptable standard of living.

5 Many families used to live in close-knit communities, with grandmothers, aunts and other relations living nearby, who were easily available to help with the care of the children. These communities are now breaking up and families may now have no close relatives living nearby to help.

6 There are cases of special need, for example, an unsupported mother, an unfortunate background of poor or overcrowded housing conditions, ill-health, mental or physical handicap, or a general inability to cope with looking after children. In such cases it is desirable to provide help for families with caring for their children.

Questions

1 **Describe briefly the kind of care children need if they are to be physically well developed and healthy.**
2 **What stages does a small child pass through as he learns to mix socially? How can a good nursery group help in this development?**
3 **Why is it important to help a young child to develop emotionally?**
4 **In what ways could you encourage the development of a small child's intelligence?**
5 **Why do you think many mothers want to go out to work, even if they do not really need the money?**
6 **In what circumstances do you think mothers really need help in caring for their children?**
7 **If you had two children under five, and enough money, would you want to go out to work? Give all the reasons you can think of.**
8 **Do you think your children would develop better in all ways if you were at home or at work?**

# Facilities for pre-school children

### Private day nurseries

These are often good but are usually rather expensive and so are most frequently used by mothers who are better off. They have to be registered with the local authority who make checks on safety, numbers, staff, hygiene facilities and so on. Many thousands of children attend these private nurseries. Sometimes they are attached to factories or colleges and are only for the use of those mothers working there. They usually cater only for children over two or three years old, and much less frequently for babies.

### Pre-school play groups

These also have to be registered with the local authority. They are normally run by some of the mothers whose children attend the group and are often held in a church hall or community centre on perhaps two or three mornings or afternoons a week. They are only part-time and provide an opportunity for the child's social development through play with others, but of course they do not provide the full daily care of the child which is required by a working mother and which is provided by a day nursery.

### Local authority day nurseries

These are usually run by the Department of Health and Social Security and are primarily concerned with the physical care of the children in their charge, as compared with nursery classes or schools whose main concern is with educational development.

Children can attend these nurseries from the age of six weeks to five years old, and they are usually open from early in the morning until the evening, to cater for mothers who have to work a full day.

There are long waiting lists for these nurseries and priority is given to mothers who for social reasons must go out to work, for example a mother who has no husband to support her and the child. Other mothers who are unable to cope with looking after their children themselves, perhaps because of poor housing or mental or physical inability to run a home and family, also have priority. This means that the ordinary mother who has no special need but would just like to go out to work often has very little chance of obtaining a place for her child in a local authority day nursery, though the number of places available varies a great deal from one area to another. There are usually more in inner city areas where there tends to be a higher number of families with greater social need.

**Nursery classes, nursery units, nursery schools**

These are run by the Department of Education and Science and are primarily concerned with encouraging intellectual development so that children have a good start when they begin compulsory schooling at five years old. They usually take children from three or four years old depending on the number of places available. Again priority is usually given to opening nursery classes in city areas, though some local authorities are trying to extend this to offer places to all who would like them.

**Child minders**

More children below school age are looked after by child minders than by any other scheme, though as these arrangements are usually privately made between individuals no exact figures are available. Child minders are encouraged to register with the local authority, so that checks can be made to cut down the possibilities of overcrowding, lack of facilities for playing, unsafe conditions and so on. Some authorities have encouraged child minders to register with them by operating a free lending service of toys, books, fireguards and other equipment and by offering help and advice.

Questions

1 **What are the advantages and disadvantages of private nurseries for a mother who wishes to return to work?**
2 **Describe how a pre-school play group is usually run.**
3 **Where would you expect to find most local authority day nurseries? Explain why.**
4 **Describe fully the services provided by a local authority day nursery.**
5 **What is the difference between a local authority day nursery and a nursery school or class?**
6 **You want to go out to work and are considering having your child looked after by a child minder. Make a list of all the points you would look for when deciding whether or not she would offer suitable care for your child.**

# Welfare services

Some of the welfare services which the State provides are outlined below. The circumstances of each case vary from family to family, so it is always advisable to consult your local branch of the Department of Health and Social Security if you think you may be eligible for any benefits. The cost of providing the services and benefits is met through the various taxes we pay and through the National Insurance contributions paid by all employed people.

*Child Benefit* (formerly Family Allowance). This is a cash sum payable weekly for all children in the family, usually to the mother. All families receive this, whatever their income. An additional sum is paid to one-parent families.

*Family Income Supplement*. This is paid to families where the breadwinner is in full-time work, where there is at least one child and where the total income is below a certain level. Single and self-employed parents may also claim. Families receiving F.I.S. are also automatically entitled to;

a   free N.H.S. prescriptions, dental treatment and glasses.
b   free milk and vitamins for expectant mothers and children under school age.
c   free school meals.
d   refund of hospital fares.
e   free legal aid and advice.

*Supplementary Benefit*. You may be entitled to this if you are not in full-time work and your income for any reason is below a certain level. If you receive Supplementary Benefit you are also entitled to many of the items in the previous paragraph and sometimes help with the cost of heating, clothing or special diets.

*Unemployment Benefit* is payable if you are unemployed but willing to work for an employer and have paid enough National Insurance contributions. There is a basic rate payable depending on the size of the family and an earnings related supplement is paid for some months, the amount varying according to your earnings before you were unemployed.

*Sickness Benefit* is payable if you are unable to work through ill-health. After a certain number of weeks, normally about 28, you would be paid invalidity benefit in its place.

*Retirement pension* is paid to men over 65 and women over 60 who have retired. You may qualify for a larger pension if you continue to work until 70 (for men) or 65 (for women). If elderly people find it difficult to manage on their income they may be entitled to a supplementary pension as well. Free prescriptions are available to men aged over 65 and to women aged over 60.

*Attendance Allowance* is for those who are severely disabled mentally or physically and who need a lot of looking after.

*Invalid Care Allowance* is for people of working age who cannot work as they have to stay at home to care for a severely disabled relative.

*Widows' Benefits* are available to widows with or without children, depending on individual circumstances.

*Maternity Benefits* – see page 149.

*Disease, injury or accident* caused through your employment could entitle you or your family to certain benefits.

*Death Grant* may be available to help with funeral expenses in cases of need.

*Mobility Allowance* is available as a cash benefit to help you to achieve greater mobility if you cannot work through physical disability. It is an alternative to an invalid vehicle for those who want it.

---

## Questions

1  **You are uncertain as to whether or not you qualify for certain welfare benefits. How would you obtain exact information about this?**
2  **Where does the money come from to pay for the welfare services?**
3  **Who is entitled to Family Income Supplement? What other benefits would a family receiving this be able to have as their right?**
4  **What benefits are available to elderly people?**
5  **Describe six other benefits provided by Britain's welfare state which you think are particularly helpful to people in need. Say why you consider each one to be important.**

# Help for handicapped people

There are many different kinds of services and cash benefits available to handicapped people, both through state schemes and through voluntary organizations. The Social Services department of the local authority usually has information about the help that is available from all sources and can advise you on your particular needs and how they can be met.

### Financial help

Some of the benefits described on pages 162–3 may be available to handicapped people. These include invalidity benefits, industrial injury and disablement benefits, attendance allowance, invalid car allowance and mobility allowance.

### Health services

The services of doctors and hospitals are provided free under the National Health Service. This may include all the cost of a long or short stay in a suitable hospital. Sometimes a short stay in hospital can be arranged, to relieve the relatives of a handicapped person for a week or two. Help with transport to and from hospital can be provided.

Help with rehabilitation is given while you are in hospital to enable you to become as independent as possible. This could include physiotherapy, which involves exercises and treatment, and occupational therapy, which teaches you how you can carry out the usual activities of washing, dressing, cooking and following your normal interests, perhaps with the help of special equipment. Speech therapy helps those whose speech has suffered through illness or disability.

### Social Services

This department of the local authority can help you cope with any kind of problem arising in the family which is caused by illness or handicap. They may help with home helps, Meals-on-Wheels, laundry, installing and paying the rent of a telephone, or providing a radio, television or books. They may also provide various aids and equipment, such as specially adapted furniture, cutlery, plates and cups and equipment designed to help with reading, writing, housework, caring for children, and gardening.

*Day centres* are provided by some local authorities, where the handicapped can take part in various activities. These may include light employment or educational handicrafts, or they may be purely social.

*Day care* for children of handicapped parents or for children with a handicap can be provided for children under school age, perhaps at a nursery, playgroup or with a registered child minder.

*Holidays and recreation*, including facilities for sport, outings, and social clubs may be available.

## Voluntary organizations

The Social Services department can put you in touch with the voluntary organizations in your area who also provide help and services of various kinds, often working in co-operation with local authorities. They, too, may lend or give equipment, and help with transport, outings, housing and social activities, or they may help with the daily tasks of changing library books, collecting pensions, doing shopping or lighting fires.

*Cheap travel* is available in some areas on buses and trains.

*Car badges* can be obtained by the disabled. These allow them to park where it would normally be restricted and to ignore the usual time limits.

*Guides for touring* are produced by some local authorities and by the A.A. with information about hotels, restaurants and places to visit in the area which make provision for the needs of handicapped people.

*Employment services* give assistance in looking for suitable employment and possible training courses.

## Housing

Financial help may be provided for adapting a council house or a privately owned house for a handicapped person. Adaptations might include moving electrical switches and sockets, or providing handrails for a bath or toilet, a downstairs toilet, an easy-to-manage heating system, wider doors and ramps for a wheelchair. Some housing is specially designed and built for those people dependent on a wheelchair. Voluntary organizations, too, may provide housing.

## Handicapped children

Parents are given advice on the most suitable kind of education available, either in an ordinary school or in a special school if the handicap is severe. Home tuition is available for children who cannot go to school.

---

Questions

1 **Where would you go for information on the help available to handicapped people?**
2 **List some of the cash benefits which may be available.**
3 **What kind of help can the handicapped receive in hospital?**
4 **Describe the different provisions made by the Social Services department for the handicapped under these headings: (a) In the home. (b) Outside the home.**
5 **What kind of services are provided by voluntary organizations?**

# The care of the elderly

## Diet

Elderly people often have a rather poor diet, which can cause a general feeling of poor health, if not actual illness. This can be due to:

1  Shortage of money.
2  Lack of knowledge about which foods will keep them feeling well.
3  Poor teeth, or dentures which do not fit well.
4  Illness, handicap, or feeling unfit, which may cause difficulty in shopping.
5  Loneliness, which may cause them to feel it is not worth taking much trouble especially if they are just cooking for one.
6  Poor cooking facilities. They may not have a refrigerator.

All these factors may result in a diet of foods which are easy to prepare and clear away and involve little cooking. Such foods are often starch – bread, cakes, biscuits – and the diet will be deficient in the protein, minerals and vitamins needed for health. The diet should be well balanced and should include sufficient:

*Protein* – easiest to digest in the form of fish, poultry, eggs and milk.

*Vitamin C* – this is good for the gums and helps in the absorption of iron. It is easily provided by fruit juice or syrup, tomatoes and green vegetables.

*Vitamin D and Calcium* – lack of these can cause a curved spine and brittle bones. They are easily provided by milk and other dairy foods.

*Iron* – lack of this can cause fatigue from lack of oxygen. It can be provided by egg yolk, liver, corned beef, red meat, dried fruit and cocoa.

## Safety

Many accidents happen to older people in their own homes, often because of poor sight, hearing or sense of balance and slower reactions. To help prevent accidents, take care to observe these general rules:

1  Good lighting is important around the house, with a bedside light for the night.
2  Floor coverings should be secure, with no loose mats or highly polished floors.
3  Firm, comfortable shoes and slippers should be worn.
4  Keep objects off the floor as far as possible.
5  Have a good handrail on the stairs.
6  Use a non-slip mat in the bath and handles beside the bath, to help elderly people to get in and out of the bath safely.
7  Avoid heaters which can be knocked over. Have heaters serviced regularly.
8  Use hot water bottles with care. Use them with covers.
9  Electric blankets should have the B.S.I. Kitemark and be regularly serviced.
10  Take particular care with pills and medicines, as old people may be forgetful.

## Housing

Housing will preferably be easy to run, clean and keep warm and safe. It should not have too many steps and stairs. It is an advantage if family, friends, shops, a post office, buses and recreational facilities are nearby.

Elderly people may like to live with their children or other relatives where they have the company of the family. If they can have a room of their own with some of their furniture and possessions, they can have some privacy and independence without feeling alone.

Flats, bungalows and homes are provided by local authorities and some voluntary organizations. They are usually specially built or adapted for the elderly. Some of these are 'sheltered', each room or flat being self-contained but with a warden who can easily be called if required by means of a bell. Sometimes these homes have a dining-room where there is an opportunity to meet and have the company of others in a similar age group.

## Financial help and welfare

Financial help of various kinds is available. This is not 'charity' but a right, because of taxes and contributions paid during your working life and still paid on goods you buy. As well as the basic retirement pension, help may be given with rent, rates, heating costs, and maintenance and insurance of the house. Many local authorities allow reduced fares or free travel to older people. Shops sometimes reduce prices of hairdressing, dry-cleaning, shoe repairs and cinema tickets.

General advice about any kind of help is available through the Social Services department, the Social Security office, the Citizens' Advice Bureau or voluntary organizations such as 'Help the Aged'. The different kinds of help may include Meals-on-Wheels, home helps, chiropodist visits, help to visit a dentist or optician, social activities such as Over 60's clubs, lunch clubs, outings and holidays.

## Health

Regular checks at the optician's and good lighting both help to prevent accidents and keep up interests and hobbies. Deafness may develop slowly, leading to a feeling of being cut off from conversations and other people. Hearing aids are free from the N.H.S. These may have extensions for television or radio. Good teeth or dentures are important for good eating and digestion. If feet are painful exercise will be reduced and it will be more difficult to keep up outside interests. Warmth is important. Older people are more likely to feel the cold if they are less active. Heating should be good, easy to manage and safe. A good diet, light, warm and easily washable clothes and bedding, woollen socks, knee caps and gloves all help in keeping warm. Pure wool is usually the warmest fibre for clothing and blankets.

Questions

1  **Describe the reasons why elderly people often have a poor diet and how they can be helped to overcome this.**
2  **What precautions could you take in your home to prevent falls?**
3  **How can older people be helped by their families to keep as fit and healthy as possible?**

# Simple first aid

A knowledge of simple first aid is very useful in treating the minor accidents which can occur at any time in the home. Prompt and correct treatment can often prevent the need for further treatment later on. If the accident is more serious, medical help should be sought at once, by taking the patient to the casualty department of a hospital or by ringing for an ambulance or doctor.

### First aid box

Every home should have a box of basic first aid equipment which is easily available when needed and yet is out of the reach of children. It should contain the following items:

Assorted sizes of plasters, or a strip
from which they may be cut
Scissors
Sterile bandages
Sterile cotton wool
A sterile dressing
Large triangular bandage
Safety pins
Anti-histamine cream
Tweezers
Thermometer

### Simple treatments

1 *Small cuts* – Clean the wound with cool, running water, dry the skin with cotton wool and cover with a clean dressing.

2 *Minor burns and scalds* – Put under cool running water to reduce the heat and relieve the pain. Dry carefully and cover loosely with a clean, dry dressing. Never cover with fat, ointments or creams.

3 *Extensive burns and scalds* – Place gently in cool running water and keep immersed for at least ten minutes. Cover loosely with a clean, dry cloth and send for medical help at once.

4 *Fainting* – If someone feels faint, get them near fresh air and give them a drink of water. Put the head between the knees so that blood can reach the brain. If someone faints, keep them lying flat. Raise the legs slightly above the level of the head. Do not make them sit up or move too soon. Loosen any clothing which is tight round the neck, chest or waist.

5 *Nosebleeds* – Tilt the head slightly forward to prevent any blood being swallowed. Gently but firmly squeeze the nostrils. Breathing should be through the mouth.

6   *Insect bites or stings* – Remove the sting with tweezers. Relieve the pain
with anti-histamine cream if you have it, or use a bicarbonate of soda solution
(or saliva) for bees and other insects. For wasp stings, apply vinegar.
Remember – 'Bicarb for bees, Winegar for wasps.'

7   *Dog bites* – If the skin has been cut, cover with a clean dressing and go to a
hospital or doctor for injections against rabies and tetanus. Try to find out who
owns the dog, so that it can be examined for disease.

8   *Poisoning* – Get medical help as soon as possible. Keep the poison so that it
can be identified and keep any vomit. Treatment varies with the type of
poison – if there are red marks around the mouth and lips, which suggest a
strong corrosive poison, do not try to make the patient sick but give him large
amounts of milk to drink (or water if no milk is available).

9   *Shock* is a physical state likely to follow any accident and can be more serious
than the injury itself. If you think there may be a fracture or internal bleeding
do not attempt to move the patient. Otherwise lay him down, make him
comfortable and reassure him. Do not put on extra clothing or rugs and do not
give any drinks.

**Home nursing**

Most people find they have to look after a sick person at home at
some time. Following these general rules will help the patient to recover.

1   Follow carefully all the doctor's instructions about diet, pills and general care.
Make a written note if necessary to help you remember.
2   Give all pills and medicines in the right amounts and at the right time.
3   Keep the patient calm and quiet. Do not allow too many visitors at first.
4   Keep the room clean, tidy, well ventilated and warm.
5   Put a paper bag for rubbish where the patient can reach it easily. It can easily
and hygienically be disposed of later.
6   Keep the bed clean and neat and the pillows fluffed up.
7   Wash the patient regularly. Brush his teeth and comb his hair. Provide
frequent changes of pyjamas or night-clothes.
8   Provide plenty of fresh water to drink.
9   Make sure the patient can call you if required by providing a small bell.
10  As he recovers, provide suitable amusement, with a radio, books, toys or
magazines. Food is important to help recovery. Doctors' instructions about
diet must be followed. Provide small meals at regular times. Serve them on a
tray laid attractively with a tray cloth, perhaps with a posy of flowers. Foods
should be easily digestible – for example, fish, chicken, and milk puddings.
Avoid spicy foods, fried foods, pork and bacon, pickles, vinegary foods, rich
cakes and pastries. All food must be scrupulously clean and fresh.

Questions

1   **What items should be kept in a first aid box at home?**
2   **What five minor accidents do you think you are most likely to have to
deal with? Describe how you would treat each one.**
3   **Describe the occasions when you would call for medical help at once.**
4   **What are the rules for home nursing?**
5   **What special care should you take when providing the patient's meals?**

# Personal hygiene

### Care of the skin

A good standard of personal hygiene helps us to resist infection and to stay healthy. Everyone should follow these normal rules of hygiene and should encourage others to do the same.

1 Hands should be washed frequently, using warm water and soap, particularly after going to the toilet and before eating meals. In our daily lives we are always touching things handled by other people, such as money, door-handles, pets, the seats of buses or trains. These can all carry tiny organisms which are transferred on to our hands and then to our food and mouths and in this way bring infection into our bodies.

2 Skin should be washed regularly to remove sweat. The easiest way to do this is by having a bath every day. If this is not possible then thorough washing with soap and warm water is just as good. It is essential to wash well under the arms every day to prevent the unpleasant smell caused by stale perspiration (sweat). Some people sweat more freely than others. They should avoid wearing nylon, polyester or other non-absorbent materials next to the skin, as this will feel uncomfortable and could cause an unpleasant smell which will be difficult to get rid of from clothes.

3 The use of deodorants and anti-perspirants can help. They should be applied to skin which is cool and clean. They work more efficiently if the hair under the arms is removed, either with a razor or with a special depilatory cream. Deodorants may simply prevent the perspiration from developing an unpleasant odour, whereas anti-perspirants prevent perspiration being produced in the part of the skin where they are applied. They can be bought as aerosol sprays, sticks, roll-on liquids or creams and may vary as to how well they work for an individual person. Some people naturally perspire more than others. They may find roll-on lotions or creams work better for them.

4   Underclothing should be clean and changed often. Cotton underwear is best and most comfortable as it is absorbent and so can soak up sweat from the surface of the skin.

### Acne

Acne is quite common in teenagers, when oil-producing glands in the skin become very active. The pores become blocked by excessive grease and bacteria multiply in the grease, producing poisons which irritate the skin and cause the characteristic blemishes or marks.

#### *What you can do to help control acne*

1   Wash your skin frequently with soap and warm water to remove grease.
2   Use clean, well-washed hands to wash your face, not a flannel or sponge which may harbour bacteria.
3   A mild antiseptic soap may be helpful.
4   Cut greasy foods out of your diet – foods such as pastry, fried foods, cream, chocolate and pork.
5   Eat plenty of fresh fruit and vegetables and drink plenty of water.
6   Do not put greasy make-up or creams on your face.
7   Your doctor may prescribe a preparation to help clear your skin.

### The care of your hair

1   Wash your hair as often as necessary to keep it clean and free from grease.
2   Brushing will smooth the hair and keep it shiny.
3   Wash your brush and comb regularly to remove grease, dead skin and dust.
4   A good diet helps to keep your hair in good condition – plenty of fresh fruit and vegetables and protein foods, but not too much greasy food.
5   Treat your hair with consideration. Do not use chemical bleaches, colourants, 'perm' lotions, sprays and so on too often. Ask the advice of a qualified hairdresser about cutting, conditioning, or colouring your hair and avoid drastic 'do-it-yourself' changes or treatments.
6   Do not use other people's combs. Dandruff is easily passed from one person to another. Like acne, it can occur when the sebaceous (oil-producing) glands of the skin are too active. It is best to ask your doctor for a special treatment shampoo.

---

Questions

1   **Why should we try to develop good standards of hygiene in ourselves and our families?**
2   **What habits of personal hygiene would you encourage in a young child you were looking after?**
3   **What are the advantages of wearing cotton clothes next to the skin?**
4   **List all the advice you could give to someone who suffered from excessive perspiration.**
5   **What encouragement and advice could you offer to a friend who has acne?**
6   **How should you care for your hair?**

# Caring for your teeth

We would all like to have perfect, strong teeth for the sake of our health, our appearance and our comfort. Decayed teeth can lead to pain, general ill-health, gum disease and digestive disorders as well as the loss of your teeth at an early age. There is a great deal you can do to keep your teeth in good condition.

### Eating the right foods

1   The right kinds of food are all-important. For the teeth to grow and develop properly you need a good supply of calcium, phosphorus and vitamins D, C and A. This means you should have plenty of the foods which contain them, including milk, cheese, eggs, fresh fruit and vegetables.

2   Crisp, crunchy foods which need chewing and biting – such as apples, crusty bread, celery, raw carrots and nuts – are good, as they encourage the supply of blood to the teeth and gums and they help to keep the teeth clean.

3   Sweet, sticky foods are responsible for a large proportion of dental decay. Avoid these foods as much as you can, especially between meals. If you must eat sweets, eat them after a meal, then brush your teeth. It is especially harmful to leave a sweet, sticky layer of food in your mouth for long periods. The bacteria which normally live there act on this layer, forming a sticky substance called <u>plaque</u> on and around the teeth. The bacteria then produce an acid which begins to dissolve the hard enamel surface of the teeth and so they start to decay. If you brush your teeth thoroughly straight after eating sweet foods then this will not happen.

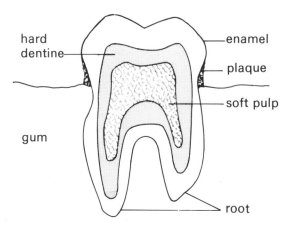

### Brushing your teeth

Regular brushing is important. Try to brush your teeth after every meal and do not eat between meals, especially sweet foods. If you cannot brush after every meal, brush at least twice a day, after breakfast and before going to bed. <u>Never</u> go to bed without brushing your teeth. Think about all the hours the bacteria will have undisturbed to set about causing your teeth to decay!

Use a fluoride toothpaste – it helps reduce decay in both adults' and children's teeth. Brush your teeth correctly, from the gum to the cutting edge of the teeth. Do not brush the gum <u>away</u> from the teeth or you will cause infection to enter between the gum and the teeth.

Have regular checks at the dentist at six-monthly intervals. He can check any decay before it gets too bad. He can also apply fluoride treatment to the teeth which helps prevent decay for several months. Another new treatment, which can protect the teeth against decay for several years, involves coating some surfaces of the teeth with a thin, plastic film.

### Fluoride

Where the mineral fluoride occurs naturally in drinking water, it has been found that children suffer much less tooth decay than in those areas where there is none. Because of this, it has been suggested that all water supplies in this country should have fluoride added to them to make up a level of one part of fluoride to one million parts of water. Other people consider that it would be wrong to force this measure upon everyone, regardless of whether they want it or not. Too much fluoride in the water can cause mottling of the teeth.

### Care of children's teeth

If you are looking after children you have a particular responsibility to help them look after their teeth.

1   Do not let them eat sweets or sweet foods between meals. Never use sweets to bribe them 'to be good', or to 'keep them quiet'. You are doing them much more harm than good in the long run.
2   Encourage them to enjoy crisp, crunchy and savoury foods rather than sweet ones.
3   Never give a baby a dummy dipped in undiluted fruit syrup.
4   Teach children to be 'grown up' and brush their teeth at an early age. Eighteen months is not too young to start. You can buy small size tooth brushes, some of which have pictures of nursery characters on them.
5   Take them for a first visit to the dentist at the age of three or four, when they will enjoy looking around. Be careful not to put the idea into their heads that going to the dentist has to be an unpleasant experience!

Questions

1   **Name five nutrients which are needed for the development of healthy teeth.**
2   **Why should you eat plenty of crisp, fibrous foods?**
3   **Explain how teeth start to decay and draw a diagram showing the structure of a tooth.**
4   **List four important points to remember about brushing your teeth.**
5   **How often should you go to the dentist for a check-up?**
6   **Explain the argument in favour of adding fluoride to drinking water.**
7   **Give as many different reasons as you can think of why it is wrong to give children sweets every time they ask for them.**

# Further work on chapter 8

1 Discuss the reasons why, and to what extent, a woman should alter her diet when she is expecting a baby.

2 Most towns will have a clinic.
(a) Explain fully three ways in which the public are helped at:
(i) ante-natal clinics; (ii) welfare clinics; (iii) school clinics;
(iv) physiotherapy clinics.
(b) What other facilities are provided for people with disabilities and where can they be obtained? (SEREB)

3 Write fully on two of the following:
(a) Buying clothes and toilet items for a new baby arriving in the spring.
(b) Preparation and giving of a bottle feed.
(c) Safety precautions to be taken in a home where a young child is just beginning to toddle. (EMREB)

4 Discuss the facilities which are available in your area for mothers with pre-school-age children. Include in your answer any financial help available. (O)

5 (a) What provisions would you hope to find for the education and care of 3–5-year-olds in your local area?
(b) In what ways can a mother prepare her child for a happy start to the infant school?
(c) What safety rules would you teach to all young children starting school? (WMEB)

6 Write on each of the following:
(a) A woman who smokes and drinks while she is pregnant.
(b) Which safety points should you look for when buying toys for a baby?
(c) A garden that is safe for a toddler.
(d) What points would you consider when choosing clothes for a baby? (EMREB)

7 (a) If you were babysitting for a small baby who woke up and started crying, what would you do?
(b) If you were looking after a toddler during the day, what safety precautions would you take in the kitchen?

8 (a) Suggest three ways in which a mother could help to ensure that her child has healthy teeth.
(b) What would you do in the following situations? (i) A friend has a nose bleed. (ii) You burn your fingers on a hot plate. (iii) An old lady trips down some steps and is lying unconscious.
(c) You have a three-year-old coming to stay. What precautions should you take to avoid accidents during her stay? (SREB)

9  How would you deal with the following accidents in the home:
   (a) fainting
   (b) a bee sting
   (c) minor burns
   (d) poisoning?

10 Your mother has to stay in bed for a few days.
   (a) What preparations should you make for the doctor's visit?
   (b) When serving her a meal in bed, how should you make sure
   she is comfortable?
   (c) When preparing meals for invalids, what points should you
   take into consideration?
   (d) Plan a two-course midday meal for your mother. (SEREB)

11 The welfare of the community is important.
   (a) Name two services which are connected with the welfare of each of
   the following: (i) babies and young children under five years of age;
   (ii) teenagers; (iii) disabled people.
   (b) State three advantages to a child of three years old attending a
   pre-school playgroup.
   (c) Explain how doctors and the general public have benefited from the
   setting up of Health Centres.
   (d) Name three groups of people who are eligible for free medicines,
   on prescription, from the chemist. (SEREB)

12 Try to arrange a visit to your local clinic and outline the range of
   services they offer to different groups of people in your community.
   Find out how much money from the rates your local authority spends
   each year on these welfare services.

13 Give two ways in which the State will help in the following situations:
   (a) a family with several children still at school
   (b) an unmarried or deserted mother and her children
   (c) a family where the father is seriously ill
   (d) the wife of a man who is in prison.

14 Various groups in the community need specific help. Write what you
   know about the Social Services and voluntary help available in three
   of the following instances:
   (a) a mother with a new baby
   (b) an old person living alone
   (c) a young couple experiencing marriage problems
   (d) a father unable to work through ill-health. (SREB)

15 What special provision is made for the health and welfare of old
   people? Include financial help in your answer. (O)

16 Your grandmother is coming to live with your family. What special
   points would you need to consider when planning a bedsitter for
   her? (O)

17 What provisions are made by the Social Services to assist disabled people to carry out a useful job and lead a reasonably active life? Describe how ordinary people can also help them. (O)

18 How would you encourage young children to take good care of their teeth and gums? Discuss methods which help prevent tooth decay. Illustrate your answers with diagrams. (O)

19 (a) What are the causes of acne?
(b) What advice would you give to a teenage boy to help him control his acne?
(c) What is dandruff?
(d) How would you get rid of dandruff?
(e) State the different ways in which greasy hair can be kept in good condition.
(f) Give four tips to a friend on how to lose weight. (O)

20 (a) Skin care is particularly important in adolescence. List four rules which a teenager should follow to ensure a healthy skin.
(b) Describe the functions of: (i) the epidermis; (ii) the dermis; (iii) the sweat glands.
(c) In what way does a deodorant differ from an anti-perspirant?
(d) Which of the properties of the fabrics used in underwear safeguard health? Give reasons for your answers. (SCE)

**Books for further reading**

Leaflets on current Social Security benefits available from Social Security offices
*Consumer's Guide to the British Social Services* **P. Willmot** Pelican
*Caring for the Elderly* **Gladys Francis** International Ideas
*Science and Your Home* **J. Gostelow** Blond Educational
*Young Student's Book of Child Care* **Pitcairn** Cambridge University Press
*Safety for your Family* **Angela Creese** Mills and Boon
*Hygiene in the Home* **Elisabeth Norton** Mills and Boon
*Introduction to Human and Social Biology* **Don Mackean and Brian Jones** John Murray

# Chapter 9
# **Feeding the family**

# Nutrition

Nutrition is the study of food and the effect it has on our bodies. The food we eat can affect us in many ways. We would all like to be healthy and slim, to have plenty of energy, a smooth, clear complexion and good teeth. We want our children to be strong and healthy. The food we eat, as growing children and as adults, plays a very important part in achieving these things.

We need food to stay alive, to be healthy and energetic. Food contains the different chemical substances – called nutrients – which our bodies need to do this properly. If our diet did not contain enough of these nutrients we would be undernourished and unhealthy. In this country, provided we eat a good variety of different foods, we are not very likely to be short of the nutrients that we need. In fact, we are more likely to eat too much of some foods and to become overweight and unhealthy.

If we have some knowledge of different foods we are more likely to be able to choose a sensible diet to suit our particular circumstances. For example, a growing child, an expectant mother, a person trying to lose weight, an old person or someone with a very strenuous job will all need rather different amounts and kinds of foods if they are to keep as fit and well as possible.

### What is food used for?

1  For the body to grow normally to adult size and for the repair and replacement of cells which are continually breaking down.

2  To provide the energy needed for all our different activities. We need energy to keep the heart beating, to enable us to digest our food, for our lungs to breathe and for the body to keep warm, as well as for such activities as walking, running, working and dancing.

3  For all the body processes to run smoothly, keeping us in good health and able to resist infection and disease.

### Some general rules for sensible eating

1  Eat as wide a variety of foods as you can. You are then unlikely to be short of any nutrient or to eat too much of another.

2  Avoid a lot of sweet foods. Jam, sweets, fizzy drinks, cakes, biscuits, chocolate, and tinned fruit in syrup are just some of the foods which contain a lot of sugar. Although they are very tempting and hard to resist altogether, try to avoid eating too many – sugary foods are bad for your health, your figure and your teeth.

3  Avoid a lot of fat in your diet. Do not spread butter too thickly on your bread – have thicker bread and thinner butter. Do not eat fried food too often, and cut down on cakes, pastry and biscuits which contain a lot of fat and sugar.

4  Eat more fresh fruit and vegetables. These give you nutrients you need and add roughage or bulk to your diet. Lack of enough fibrous food or roughage will cause constipation, and may also cause more serious disorders.

5  Eat more cereal foods. Choose breakfast cereals containing the whole grain of the wheat, or with bran, and eat more wholemeal bread. These foods also add fibrous material to the diet, whereas refined cereals and white flour have had most of the roughage removed during processing.

Questions

1  **Name some of the ways in which the food we eat can affect us.**
2  **What are nutrients?**
3  **Why should you try to eat a wide variety of foods?**
4  **Why do you think it is worth learning about foods?**
5  **What are the purposes for which the body needs food?**
6  **Name some of the foods you should try to eat less of.**
7  **What foods should you try to eat plenty of?**

# Nutrients

The different nutrients found in food are:

Protein
Carbohydrate
Fat
Minerals
Vitamins

Roughage is not a nutrient, but it is an important part of food, as it hel
food pass through your body.

**Protein**

1   Protein is needed for the growth of all the body's cells. Bones, muscles, bloo
and so on all contain protein. It is especially important that growing children
and expectant mothers have enough protein in their diet.
2   Adults need protein even when fully grown, for the continual replacement an
repair of these cells.
3   Protein can also be used as a source of energy.

*Which foods contain protein?*
Nearly all foods contain some protein. Good sources of protein are:

*From animals*
Meat, fish
Eggs
Milk
Cheese

*From plants*
Soya beans
Nuts, e.g. peanuts
Peas, beans, lentils
Bread, flour and other cereals

Soya beans may be used to produce T.V.P. (Textured Vegetable
Protein). This is processed until it resembles meat in texture and flavour and i
used quite widely in school meals, canteens, hospitals and similar places. It is
also sold in the shops to use at home as a substitute for meat. It is
nutritionally as good for you as meat but less expensive.

**Carbohydrates**

Carbohydrate foods can be divided into three main groups: sugars,
starches, and cellulose. Sugars and starches provide us with the energy we
need for all our activities. Cellulose is not used as a food but is a good source
of roughage – it forms the fibrous part and outer skins of fruit, vegetables, an
cereals.

*Which foods contain carbohydrate?*
Sugars – sugar, jam, sweets, syrup
Starches – potatoes, flour, bread, cakes, biscuits, pastry
Cellulose – fruit, vegetables, cereals, bran

**Fats**

Fat is a useful food in the diet for several reasons:

1  It is a very good source of energy.
2  It contains Vitamins A and D (in animal fats).
3  The layer of fat around the body helps keep us warm.
4  Fat protects some internal organs, e.g. the kidneys, from damage.
5  A meal which contains fat keeps you feeling full for longer.
6  Foods cooked in fat, e.g. roast meat or fried fish, have a good flavour.

*Which foods contain fat?*
Butter, margarine, lard, dripping, and suet.
Vegetable oils used for cooking.
Cheese, cream, egg, fat on meat and bacon, fat in cakes and pastry.

Too much fat in the diet, though, is not good for you. It can make you overweight and can encourage greasy hair, spots and acne. It is also thought to be one of the factors causing heart disease. A mixture of fats from both vegetable and animal sources is best.

**Minerals**

*Calcium*
Calcium is needed together with phosphorus, Vitamin D and Vitamin C so that bones and teeth can develop properly. Shortage of calcium results in rickets and poor teeth. Good sources of calcium in the diet are milk, cheese, white bread, eggs, and green vegetables.

*Iron*
Iron is needed for the proper formation of the red blood cells. A lack of iron in the diet will cause poor general health and anaemia – weakness, lack of energy, shortness of breath. Good sources of iron are liver and kidney, red meat, corned beef, curry, bread, treacle, dried fruit and green vegetables.

---

Questions

1  **Why is it important to eat sufficient protein? Name some good sources of protein.**
2  **Suggest some ways of cutting down on the amount of fat in your daily diet.**
3  **Name some very sugary foods. Why should you avoid eating a lot of them?**
4  **What is the main advantage of eating foods containing a lot of fibre? Give some examples of these foods.**
5  **What is T.V.P.? Why is it widely used in schools and canteens?**
6  **Copy the chart on page 184 into your exercise book. List the six foods which appear most often on the chart as good sources of different nutrients.**
7  **Suggest meals for one day for a family which would give them a good supply of iron-rich foods.**

# Vitamins

Vitamins are chemical substances found in food. We need only tiny amounts, but they are essential for normal growth and development in children, for general good health and resistance to disease.

### Vitamin A – Retinol

This is a fat-soluble vitamin (found in fats). It is needed for:
1 Normal growth of children, especially bones and teeth.
2 Keeping the mucous membranes, e.g. in the throat, in healthy condition so that they can resist infection.
3 Healthy eyes, good vision in dim light.

It is found in:

| *Animal foods* | *Plant foods* |
|---|---|
| Liver – cod-liver oil | In the form of <u>carotene</u> which is converted |
| Margarine, dairy foods | to Vitamin A in the body. In carrots and other |
| Oily fish | orange/yellow and green vegetables and fruit. |

### Vitamin D – Cholecaciferol

This is also fat-soluble. It is needed so that calcium and phosphorus (see minerals) can be properly absorbed and used to make strong bones and teeth. If there is not enough Vitamin D in the diet children may develop rickets, a bone disease causing bow legs and knock knees.

It is found in oily fish, cod-liver oil, liver, margarine, butter and eggs.

*Sunlight*

The action of sunlight on the skin causes Vitamin D to be formed under the skin. This is why rickets is more often found in cool, cloudy climates than in sunny ones, or in industrial areas where heavy pollution of the air prevents the sun's rays from reaching the skin.

It is particularly important that young babies have enough Vitamin D to form their growing bones and teeth, and it is usual to give them a Vitamin D preparation bought from the local clinic. It is important to give the baby the correct amount, usually one or two drops, as too much Vitamin D is poisonous.

### The Vitamin B group

This contains several different water-soluble vitamins, including: $B_1$ Thiamin, $B_2$ Riboflavin, and $B_3$ Niacin. They are needed for:
1 Growth and good health.
2 Releasing the energy from carbohydrate foods.
3 A healthy nervous system.

They are found in small amounts in a wide variety of foods, particular natural, unprocessed foods. Some good sources are wholemeal flour, wholegrain cereals, liver and kidney, yeast and yeast extract, meat and eggs.

## Vitamin C – Ascorbic acid

Vitamin C is water-soluble.

It is needed for:

1 Healthy skin and body tissues.
2 It helps iron to be absorbed into the body.
3 It helps in the healing of wounds.
4 Healthy teeth and gums.

It is found in fresh fruit and vegetables. Some good sources are:

Oranges and other citrus fruits
Blackcurrants
Rose-hip syrup

Potatoes
Green vegetables
Tomatoes

Vitamin C is easily destroyed while food is being prepared and cooked; it dissolves out into cooking water, it is destroyed by heat, and it is destroyed by oxidation (exposure to the air). To make sure that vegetables and fruit lose as little Vitamin C as possible, the following rules must be carefully followed:

1 Use vegetables and fruit which are as fresh as possible. Do not store them for long.
2 Do not leave them to soak.
3 Put them into a small amount of boiling water and cook for as short a time as possible with the lid on. Use the cooking liquid for gravy.
4 Serve as quickly as possible. Do not keep vegetables hot for long periods.

---

### Questions

1 **Name two fat-soluble vitamins and some foods you would expect to contain plenty of them.**
2 **Name two water-soluble vitamins.**
3 **What is carotene?**
4 **Why could Vitamin D be called the sunshine vitamin?**
5 **What kind of foods are likely to be good sources of B vitamins?**
6 **Why should you eat plenty of fresh fruit and vegetables?**
7 **Describe how you would prepare and cook fresh cabbage in order to conserve as much Vitamin C as possible.**

# Summary

| Nutrient | Functions in the body | Good sources in the diet |
|---|---|---|
| *Protein* | For growth and repair of tissues. A secondary source of energy. | *Animal* – meat, fish, cheese, eggs, milk<br>*Vegetable* – soya beans, nuts, cereals, pulses |
| *Carbohydrate* | Source of energy for all the body's activities.<br>Cellulose provides roughage, although it is not a food. | *Sugars* – sugar, treacle, syrup, jam, honey, fruit<br>*Starches* – flour (e.g. in bread, cakes, puddings), other cereals, potatoes<br>*Cellulose* – fruit, vegetables, bran, wholemeal bread, whole cereals |
| *Fat* | A very good source of energy. A layer of fat insulates the body, preventing the loss of heat. Some organs of the body, e.g. the kidneys, are protected by fat. Animal fats contain Vitamins A and D. Keeps you feeling 'full' after a meal – it has a 'high satiety value'. | *Animal* – milk, butter, cream, cheese, suet, fatty meat, oily fish<br>*Vegetable* – margarines, salad or cooking oils |
| **Mineral** | | |
| *Iron* | Needed to form the red blood cells which carry the necessary oxygen to all parts of the body. Lack of iron may cause <u>anaemia</u>. | Liver, kidney, red meat, corned beef<br>Curry, green vegetables, bread, cocoa, treacle, dried fruit |
| *Calcium* | Development of strong bones and teeth, together with phosphorus, Vitamins D, C and A.<br>Needed for clotting of blood. | Milk, cheese, eggs<br>Fish bones, e.g. salmon<br>Added to white bread |
| *Phosphorus* | Strong bones and teeth. | Present in most proteins |

| Vitamin | Functions in the body | Good sources in the diet |
|---|---|---|
| A *(Retinol)* fat-soluble | Normal growth of children, especially bones and teeth. Keeps mucous membranes healthy. Healthy eyes, vision in dim light. | *Animal* – fish-liver oil, oily fish, liver, dairy foods, margarine *Plant foods* – as carotene, in orange/yellow fruit and vegetables. Green vegetables. |
| D *(Calciferol)* fat-soluble | Works with calcium and phosphorus to form strong teeth and bones. Prevents rickets. | *Animal* – similar sources to Vitamin A, though rather less in dairy foods. Sunlight acting on the fat layer under the skin forms Vitamin D. |

**Vitamin B complex**

| | | |
|---|---|---|
| B$_1$ *Thiamine* | For growth of children and good health. Helps liberate the energy from carbohydrate foods. Healthy nervous system. | Found in a variety of 'natural', unprocessed foods. Wholemeal flour, whole cereals Yeast, yeast extract (Marmite) Meat, liver, eggs |
| B$_2$ *Riboflavin* | Similar to B$_1$. | Similar to B$_1$, also a useful amount in milk. |
| B$_3$ *Niacin or Nicotinic acid* | Similar to B$_1$ and B$_2$. | Similar to B$_1$ and B$_2$. Milk products do not provide much. |

| | | |
|---|---|---|
| **Vitamin C** *(Ascorbic acid)* | Normal growth of children. Clear skin, healthy tissues. Healing of wounds. Healthy teeth and gums. Helps absorption of iron. Prevents scurvy. | *Fruit* – blackcurrants, rose-hip syrup Citrus fruits – oranges, lemons, grapefruit Tomatoes, potatoes, fresh green vegetables |

This is the vitamin most likely to be lacking in the diet in this country.

# Shopping for food

When you are working out your family budget, you will decide how much you can spend on food. Try to spend the full amount actually <u>on</u> food; personal spending money for items like magazines, tights, cosmetics or sweets should be kept in a separate purse. Money spent on food is money well spent on your family's good health. There are many ways in which you can make sensible economies without cutting down on the nutritional value of your food.

**Sensible ways to save money**

1   Plan a week's meals in advance and you will be able to work out exactly how much you need to buy.

2   Make a shopping list of the things you need. Do not stick to it too strictly if there are any good offers which would be really useful to you.

3   Look out for 'special offers', but be careful. Ask yourself, is the article something you would have bought anyway? Do you really need it? Is it really much cheaper?

4   Get to know the usual prices of foods, then you will know whether a special offer is really much cheaper.

5   Do not go shopping too often. If you do your main shopping once a week, you may only need to go shopping again for fresh meat and bread and you will avoid the temptations of buying things you can really do without.

6   You can 'shop around', as costs for the same foods will vary from one shop to another. Whether you will want to do this will depend on the time and energy you have to spare.

7   Buy fruit and vegetables when they are in season as they will be cheap, plentiful and good — and you can find out just by looking carefully at the greengrocers. Cheaper fruit and vegetables are as good for you as more expensive ones. Cabbage, turnips and carrots, for example, are as good as cauliflower, mushrooms and peppers. If you live near a market you may find their fruit and vegetables are really fresh and quite a lot cheaper.

Look for fruit for making your own jams and marmalade – it will taste good and can be cheaper. Plum jam (late summer), rhubarb and ginger jam (early summer), blackberry and apple jelly (autumn) and marmalade are all cheap to make and delicious to eat.

8   Know which kinds of meat are cheaper. There are plenty of cookery books to give you ideas for appetizing meals using cheaper cuts of meat. Meat is usually cheaper because it is tougher or has more fat or bone, so you will have to consider whether or not it will be a better buy. Planning meals ahead will give you time to prepare and cook. A pressure cooker or a slow cooker is very good for tenderizing tougher cuts of meat. Cooking stews or casseroles with plenty of vegetables, or adding stuffing, rice, dumplings and so on all help meat to go further.

Use eggs, cheese, or soya protein to make a main dish sometimes, as a substitute for meat.

9   Look for cheaper fish – mackerel and herring are cheap, as are tinned pilchards, and they are all good for you. Try a cheaper white fish such as coley or rock salmon. Cook them with a sauce, fry them, make a fish pie or fish cakes for a nutritious meal.

10   Home-made bread, cakes, scones and biscuits can be cheaper than bought ones and usually taste much better. Although it can take a lot of time, many people enjoy baking and nearly everyone enjoys eating home-baked food! Choose recipes carefully if you are trying to save money, otherwise it can be expensive. Remember also that cakes and pastries are a luxury rather than a necessity and that too many are not good for you or your figure.

11   If you have a freezer you can freeze fresh fruit and vegetables from your garden or when they are cheap to buy. (See page 96.) Meat, fish and vegetables from frozen food centres are often cheaper than fresh produce. You do not have to own a freezer to take advantage of their lower prices.

12   The most important thing to remember when trying to save on food bills is to spend your money on the foods which are best for you. Buy protein foods (meat, fish, milk, eggs and cheese), bread, fruit, vegetables and cereals. You can safely cut down on pastry, biscuits, cakes, chocolate, tinned fruit, cream, fruit squashes and crisps, foods which you may enjoy but are probably better without anyway.

---

Questions

1   **What are the advantages and disadvantages of making a shopping list and sticking to it?**
2   **What are the disadvantages of shopping daily?**
3   **What should you consider before buying 'special offers'?**
4   **How can you give your family plenty of fruit and vegetables without spending too much money?**
5   **Is it always economical to buy cheaper cuts of meat? Why?**
6   **If you were trying to save money, what foods would you (a) try to include in meals, and (b) feel you could safely cut down on?**

# Convenience foods

'Convenience foods' are foods where some of the preparation or cooking of fresh ingredients has been done by the manufacturer before we buy them. A hundred years ago, there were very few available and all meals had to be prepared from fresh ingredients. Now there are hundreds of tins, packets, jars and frozen foods on the shelves of the supermarkets.

| *Some convenience foods* | *Their fresh equivalent* |
| --- | --- |
| Packet or tinned soup. | Soup made at home from fresh vegetables, meat and stock. |
| Tinned or frozen meat and fish. Ready-cooked frozen meals, e.g. cooked beef in gravy. Packets of dried 'ready-meals', e.g. curry and rice, chicken risotto. | Fresh meat or fish from the butcher or fishmonger. |
| Bottled jam, marmalade, sauces and pickles. | Home-made jams, etc., using fresh fruit, vegetables and other ingredients. |
| Packet mixes for cakes, scones, pastry, cheesecake, trifle and batters. | Home-baked foods made from eggs, flour, sugar, margarine. |
| Instant dessert whips, creamy toppings, tinned custard, pie fillings. | Sweets made with cream, fruit, sugar, milk and eggs. |
| 'Instant' potato, freeze-dried vegetables. | Fresh vegetables. |
| Packet sauce mixes, canned sauces for cooking meat casseroles. | Sauces made from a variety of different ingredients. |
| Frozen pastry, cakes, vegetables, pies, ice-cream. | |

## Using convenience foods in cookery

Sometimes fresh foods cost more than convenience foods, sometimes less. The flavour of home-made foods is very often better, but they may take much longer to prepare. This can be important especially if a housewife goes out to work, or if visitors call unexpectedly. Even an unskilled cook can prepare an appetizing meal with the help of some packets or cans, while a good cook will find them useful to add variety to meals.

Convenience foods can usually be stored for some length of time. It is useful to have a store in the cupboard for emergencies, perhaps when illness prevents you from shopping or cooking, or for visitors. From the point of view of health, variety, flavour and economy it is best to include as many fresh foods in your meals as you can, using convenience foods as useful 'extras'.

The food value of convenience foods is usually as good as the fresh equivalent, especially the protein, fat, carbohydrate and minerals which remain much the same. The vitamin which is most easily lost, vitamin C, is usually present in canned and frozen fruit and vegetables in amounts about equal to those in fresh foods. Only the best fruit and vegetables are used by manufacturers for canning and freezing. They are usually picked and processed quickly and need only a short cooking or reheating time at home. By the time fresh food has been bought, stored, prepared and cooked at home, the vitamin C content is much the same.

## Additives to food

Many of the hundreds of different foods we see on the shelves in shops have chemicals added to them, to improve their colour, texture, flavour or appearance and to help lengthen their 'shelf-life'. We call these 'food additives'. Without them and without the chemicals used when food is grown it would not be possible to produce the amount and variety of food we use today.

As these additives are so widely used it is important to use them with caution, and the Food Standards Committee in Britain states which additives may be used and in what amounts. Different countries do not always agree about safe additives, but a lot of care and research goes into making sure that the food we eat is as free as possible from any substances which may be harmful to us.

Questions

1 **What are convenience foods? List some ideas for dishes you could make which combine both fresh and convenience foods as ingredients.**
2 **What are the advantages of using convenience foods?**
3 **How does processing affect the nutritional value of foods?**
4 **Look at the labels on some packets, jars, and tins of food. Make a list of any of the contents which you would call 'food additives'.**
5 **Some people say that 'there are too many chemicals in food today'. Do you agree? Give your reasons.**
6 **Using a recipe book work out the cost of making (a) a sandwich cake, (b) scones, (c) a jar of jam and (d) potatoes for four people. Then compare this with the cost of buying the equivalent convenience food. Remember to compare equal amounts.**

# Planning meals

It is always a good idea to plan your meals for a week in advance if you can. It will cut down the time spent on shopping, and will save you money if you go to the shops knowing exactly what you need.

When you are planning the meals, think about these points:

1   Is the meal well balanced, providing the nutrients you need? Plan the protein part of the meal first (meat, fish, cheese, eggs) and make sure you include some fresh fruit or vegetables in every meal.

2   A family may include people with different needs – perhaps an old person, small children, a man with a heavy manual job and a large appetite, someone on a slimming diet or an expectant mother. You should to try to choose meals which can be adapted to suit the needs of the members of your own family.

3   When you are out shopping, notice which foods – fruit and vegetables especially – are in season, and choose them. They will be at their best and cheapest then.

4   The money you have to spend will influence the foods you buy. Remember that cheaper cuts of meat, carefully cooked with plenty of vegetables, will give you just as nourishing and tasty a meal as more expensive cuts.

5   Consider the time you have for preparing and cooking meals. If you are out at work all day you will have less time to spend. A pressure cooker, an automatic oven or a slow cooker could be very useful. A freezer would mean that some of the meals for the week ahead could be prepared in advance and frozen. Tinned, packet and frozen foods save preparation time and can add variety to your meals. They can be as cheap as fresh foods and are very useful, but you should prepare meals from fresh foods as often as possible.

6   Try to be economical with fuel – if you are putting the oven on, bake several dishes at once. With careful planning you can make meals using the cooker top only.

7   The meals you plan should be suitable for the time of the year and the weather. Warm, filling dishes, such as stews and casseroles, will be appetizing in cold weather, salads and cold sweets will be more suitable in summer.

## Meals for small children (about 2–5 years)

Although toddlers are growing, they often have small appetites. Because of this it is advisable to give them small portions of the foods which are good for them, being careful not to give them too many starchy foods which they do not need. Food should be easy to chew and digest and not too difficult to manage on a plate. Highly spiced or seasoned foods or large amounts of fried foods cannot be easily digested by a small child and should therefore be avoided.

Try to encourage children to like a wide variety of foods. Serve small portions, attractively presented. China decorated with nursery characters is usually very popular with children, and specially shaped cutlery and dishes make it easier for them to manage food on their own.

Do not allow children to eat between meals especially if they have a poor appetite. A drink of milk or fruit juice should be enough. Sweets between meals should never be allowed or used as a bribe for good behaviour. If you want your children to have sweets, give them after meals and then help them to brush their teeth. Sweet, sticky foods will cause tooth decay. If you want your children to have good, strong teeth it is up to you to encourage good habits from an early age. Crisp, crunchy foods, like apples, raw carrots, and crusts, will help their teeth and gums. Training in good table manners can start early too, with the good example set by adults.

### Suitable meals for one day for a toddler

| Breakfast | Lunch | Tea |
|---|---|---|
| Cereal or porridge, milk | Minced beef | Sandwiches (e.g. cheese, |
| Scrambled or boiled egg | Mashed potatoes | egg and cress, sardine, |
| Toast, butter | Carrots and peas | yeast extract) |
| Milk to drink | Stewed apple | Milk pudding with |
| | Custard | blackcurrant or rose-hip syrup |
| | Milk to drink | Sponge cake or biscuit |
| | | Milk or fruit juice to drink |

Include a pint of milk every day.

## Older children

Children who are still growing quickly need a good diet with good helpings of protein and dairy foods, fruit and vegetables and enough fats and carbohydrates to provide the increasing amounts of energy they need.

## Adolescents

Boys in particular need more food at this time than at any other during their life, as they are growing and developing rapidly. Good helpings of protein foods, fruit and vegetables are needed. Fat will provide them with a concentrated source of energy without their having to eat large quantities of carbohydrates which would make the diet too bulky. Foods rich in iron are important for both girls and boys at this age.

Questions

1 **Do you think it is worth planning meals for a week ahead? What advantages does this have?**
2 **What do you consider the five most important points to bear in mind when you are choosing meals for your family?**
3 **What equipment could a working housewife buy to save time spent on cooking/serving meals?**
4 **Why should you look out for fruit and vegetables which are in season?**
5 **Do you think it is kind to give children plenty of sweets when they ask for them, or to keep them quiet? Why?**
6 **List six points to remember when choosing meals for toddlers.**
7 **Plan suitable meals for one day for a three-year-old child. Use a recipe book for ideas if it will help you.**

# Feeding adults

## Manual workers

Manual workers doing heavy work which uses a lot of physical energy need extra foods to supply that energy. Extra portions of bread, potatoes, fried food, cakes and pastry will provide this.

## Expectant mothers

See chapter 8, page 146.

## Invalids

In certain cases the doctor will prescribe a special diet which must be carefully followed. Those people who are unwell or recovering from an illness but are not on a special diet should have a suitable diet to help their recovery.

Protein foods are needed to help repair tissues, with plenty of foods to provide the minerals and vitamins needed for good health. Large amounts of carbohydrates and fats are unnecessary as an invalid does not use much energy. Fatty, greasy foods should be avoided altogether, as should highly spiced foods which could be indigestible.

Meals for invalids should be attractively served, as their appetite may not be very good. (See chapter 8, page 169.)

### Suitable dishes for an invalid

| Breakfast | Main meals | Puddings, tea |
|---|---|---|
| Fruit juice | Steamed, baked | Milk puddings, |
| Cereal and milk | or grilled white fish | such as rice |
| Milky porridge | with sauce | or semolina |
| Boiled, poached | Chicken, rabbit, liver, | Baked egg custard |
| or scrambled egg | lamb or beef. These may | Stewed fruit |
| Toast, bread and butter | be stewed in a casserole | Light sponge puddings |
| Honey, marmalade | or grilled. | Light sponge cake |
| Tea (not strong) | Avoid fried meat | Plain biscuits |
| | and rich sauces. | Bread and butter |
| | Potatoes and vegetables | Fresh fruit |

## Elderly people

As they get older, people may find that food becomes less easy to digest. Some gradual changes in eating habits will help avoid indigestion. A well-balanced diet is important if they are to feel as healthy and fit as possible. The foods which are suitable for invalids, listed above, will often suit older people too. (See also chapter 8, page 166.)

## Vegetarians

Vegetarians are people who will not eat animal flesh. There are several reasons why people choose to be vegetarians. They may feel that eating meat is a wasteful use of the world's food supplies when much of the world's population is hungry and underfed. If all agricultural land was used to produce food crops, rather than to raise animals for meat, then many more people could be fed adequately. Other people are vegetarians because they find the idea of eating animal flesh distasteful or because they feel healthier if they do not eat meat.

Some vegetarians are very strict and will not eat any animal products, including milk and eggs. Their main sources of protein are nuts, pulse vegetables such as lentils, and soya bean products. Others are lacto-vegetarians, who will not eat animal flesh but will eat eggs, milk and cheese. It is easier to provide them with a good, varied diet.

Some firms specialize in producing foods for vegetarians, for example nut rissoles or lentil cutlets. There are plenty of recipe books full of ideas for vegetarian dishes. They use different pulses (peas, beans, lentils) or nuts, rice or other cereals, in place of meat, egg or cheese dishes. Health food shops usually sell a variety of these foods, not only to vegetarians but to anyone who enjoys unrefined whole foods.

*Suitable dishes for lacto-vegetarians*
Cheese and vegetable flans, pies or turnovers
Vegetable curry, egg curry
Cheese pizza
Cheese pudding
Stuffed eggs, stuffed tomatoes
Eggs in cheese sauce
Omelettes
Cauliflower cheese
Macaroni cheese
Mixed vegetables in cheese sauce
Cheese soufflé

*Suitable dishes for vegans (strict vegetarians)*
Vegetable pies and curries
Nut roast
Nut rissoles
Peppers, courgettes, tomatoes etc. stuffed with rice
Vegetable soups
Salads
Vegetable stews
Mushroom rissoles

Questions
1 **Plan suitable meals for one day (breakfast, dinner and tea) for:**
a **a manual worker**
b **a person recovering from 'flu**
c **an old lady**
2 **List the possible reasons why someone might become a vegetarian.**
3 **Plan meals for one day for a vegetarian who will eat eggs, milk and cheese.**
4 **What kinds of protein can strict vegetarians eat?**

# Losing weight and staying slim

Being overweight is not good for your health or appearance. It can make you feel unfit, tired, short of breath, and it puts an extra strain on the heart. Clothes cannot look attractive if they are bursting at the seams and it is depressing to have to buy larger sizes than you know you ought to take.

## Are you overweight?

Most of us know when we are putting on weight – our clothes feel tight, we have a spare tyre (or several!) and layers of extra fat. There are plenty of charts showing your ideal weight, according to your sex, age, height and frame. Many people who are overweight put it down to all sorts of reasons – they say that it 'runs in the family' or that they have 'heavy bones' or are 'getting older'. The simple fact is that we get fat because we eat more food than the body needs, and the excess food is turned to fat.

Always consult your doctor if you are unsure whether or not you should try to slim, or how to do it. Remember that slimming too fast can make you ill. The condition of anorexia nervosa is becoming increasingly common among teenage girls trying to lose weight.

## Calories

The energy (and fattening!) value of foods can be measured in calories. We need a certain number of calories according to our basic size and the work we do. For example a girl of about 15 or 16 will use about 2300 calories (9.6 MJ or megajoules) per day. It is when we take in more calories than we need that fat is formed. When people talk about a 'calorie-controlled diet' they mean that they plan their day's meals so that the calorie intake from their food is less than their body requires. This means that some of the fat in the body is used up to provide their calories, and so they lose fat.

If you are really keen to diet methodically, you can buy calorie charts very cheaply. These tell you the exact calorific value of most foods so that you can work out a diet to suit yourself. You must keep to 1200–1500 calories (5.0–6.3 MJ) daily if you want to lose weight at a safe, steady pace.

## Foods high in calories which you should avoid

These are two main types:

*Fatty foods* – butter, margarine, lard, oil, cream, pastry, fried foods, crisps.

*Sugary foods* – sugar, jam, marmalade, chocolate, sweets, fruit squashes, tinned fruit, cakes, biscuits.

*Bread and potatoes* are good for you, so you should eat reasonable amounts. It is the butter you put on them, or the fat or oil you fry chips in, which is most fattening and least good for you.

*Cheese*. Many people go on diets and start eating lots of cheese, thinking it is 'slimming'. Although it is good for you, cheese is high in calories, so have no more than 1–2 oz (25–50 g) daily.

*Milk* is good for you, so have half a pint daily. You could also use dried or fresh skimmed milk which has half the calories of fresh milk.

*Meat*. Some meats have lower calorific value than others. Avoid any fatty meat and do not fry meat.

| *Best choices for slimmers* | *More fattening meats* |
|---|---|
| Chicken | Pork |
| Liver, kidney | Sausages |
| Corned beef | Bacon |
| Lean beef, lamb | Ham |
| White fish | |

*Fruit and vegetables* are good for you as they provide nutrients you need to keep you fit and healthy, but are low in calories. Eat plenty of them. They will help you feel full, which is useful if you are eating less than usual.

### Some rules for losing weight

1. Have good helpings of protein foods, fruit, and vegetables, which you need to keep healthy. You cannot enjoy being slim unless you feel lively and energetic as well.
2. Remember to avoid fatty and sugary foods.
3. If you have a 'sweet tooth', try to gradually cut down your taste for sugar. Artificial sweeteners (saccharin) could help.
4. Some substitute foods could be useful, for example, skimmed milk instead of fresh, low-fat spread instead of butter or margarine, yeast extract instead of jam and marmalade.
5. Try to keep busy. You are often tempted to eat – and especially to eat fattening chocolates, sweets, cakes and biscuits – when you are bored or have nothing very interesting to do.
6. Try to get used to smaller portions. Your stomach will become accustomed to this and you will gradually need to eat less to feel full.
7. Eating slowly is very helpful. Fat people often tend to gulp their food down quickly, hardly noticing or enjoying the taste. Thin people often eat slowly. It helps them notice when they are feeling full and they stop eating sooner.
8. Eating small meals often may be easier than eating only three main meals a day, and this may stop you from feeling too hungry in between.

Questions

1. **Why do you think it is better to avoid being overweight?**
2. **How does a calorie-controlled diet work?**
3. **What <u>kind</u> of foods should a slimmer avoid? Give several examples.**
4. **What advice would you give a slimmer about eating**
   **(a) bread and potatoes, (b) meat, and (c) fruit and vegetables?**
5. **Which five rules would be most useful to you if you wanted to slim?**

# Food presentation

### Food for parties

Party food is usually served as a buffet meal. This means that the food is laid out on a table and guests take a plate and help themselves. The table should be laid attractively; try using a plain, brightly-coloured cloth, or crêpe paper. You can buy paper napkins in many attractive colours to match. You can make a decoration for the centre of the table, using candles or flowers in colours to go with the cloth and napkins. Plates, glasses and cutlery for serving and eating will be needed.

A bowl or jug of home-made punch looks attractive. It can be made from lemonade, fruit juice, orange squash, cold tea and ice cubes.

Food should be easy to manage with one hand as it may be eaten standing up, or on a plate balanced on your knee. There should be a choice of sweet and savoury items and a drink. Here are some suggestions:

*Savoury* – sausage rolls; vols-au-vent, with a filling such as chopped hard-boiled egg or chicken in white sauce; sandwiches with different fillings, which could be marked with a sandwich 'flag'; open sandwiches; cheese pizza; savoury flans and pies of any kind, perhaps cheese and onion, bacon and egg, chicken and mushroom, sausage and tomato; salads.

*Sweets* – individual milk jellies, mousses, cheesecake, a decorated cake, sponge flans, fresh fruit salad, fruit in jelly.

### Packed meals and picnics

As these meals have to be carried around it is all too easy to choose too many starchy foods like bread, pies and biscuits and to neglect the protein foods, fruit, and vegetables which make a meal nutritionally better for you. This is particularly important for people who have a packed lunch every day. When you are preparing packed meals, remember these points:

1 Make sure you have a good helping of protein food (meat, eggs, cheese, fish).
2 Always have some fresh fruit or salad vegetables.
3 Choose foods which are easy to pack and carry.
4 Wrap them carefully, so they will not break up, spill or dry out. Suitable wrappings are plastic bags, foil, and plastic lunch boxes.
5 Provide a drink, perhaps tea, coffee, hot chocolate, a fruit drink, or soup.
6 For a picnic, do not forget salt, pepper, cutlery, and paper napkins or tissues.

*Suitable foods*

Cold cooked chicken or meat, hard-boiled eggs, cheese. Sandwiches filled with these or with tinned fish or salad. Sausage rolls, pies in foil dishes. Salad vegetables, such as tomatoes, celery, cucumber. Fresh fruit. Milk jelly, fruit jelly in small containers, fruit pies. Plain cakes, scones or biscuits.

### Laying the table

1 See that the tablecloth or mats are clean and well ironed. You may also need thick mats to prevent hot dishes marking the table.
2 Check that cutlery and glasses are not smeared. Rub them with a soft cloth.

3 If you have flowers on the table, arrange them in a low vase or bowl so that people can talk to each other without having to peer around the vase.

4 Remember the salt, pepper, mustard, glasses, a jug of cold water, and also napkins and serving spoons and forks if you are having the meal more formally served at the table.

5 Learn to lay a place setting correctly. Here is a place correctly laid for a meal of soup, meat, vegetables and a pudding.

## Table decorations

You can make your own decoration for the centre of the table quite easily, as an attractive centre-piece for a special occasion, perhaps for Christmas, a child's birthday party or a silver wedding. You need only a little time and a few simple materials.

| Christmas | Silver wedding | Child's birthday | Small decoration |
|---|---|---|---|
| Holly, ivy | Silver cake board | Tin covered | Glass dish |
| Laurel leaves | White/silver ribbon | in crêpe paper | Coloured water |
| Tinsel | Silver baubles | or cake frill | Candle |
| Small baubles | White flowers, | Toilet roll centre | Flower heads |
| Red ribbon | green leaves | or tube of | |
| Red candle | Silver-painted | coloured card | |
| Glitter, 'snow' | leaves | Animals cut from card | |
| Base of wood, | | Crêpe paper top | |
| or flat dish. | | Ribbons | |

Other useful materials you could use include glue, scissors, crêpe paper, plasticine, flat plates, bowls and sellotape. Potatoes or 'Oasis' can be used to push firm flower stalks into, to keep them moist and in position. Candles can be stood in bottle tops and glued to a base.

Questions

1 **Make a list of foods you could make yourself to serve at an engagement party.**

2 **Suggest a suitable meal to take**

a **on a long train journey.**

b **on a day's hike in the country.**

3 **List six important points to remember when you are laying the table for a special occasion.**

4 **Design a simple table decoration for a child's party. List the materials you would need to make it.**

# Food hygiene

**Food poisoning**

Food poisoning can be caused by unhygienic handling of food. We ca
see visible dust and dirt on food but it is the bacteria we cannot see which
may be most harmful. Food poisoning can cause headaches, cramp, sicknes:
diarrhoea, weakness and even death.

*Bacteria*

Bacteria are tiny, living organisms which are all around us, in our
bodies, in food, in everything we touch. Not all bacteria are harmful, indeed
many of them are necessary to us. They increase in number very rapidly und
the right conditions, and it is when they are present in large numbers in the
food we eat that they cause illness.

*Conditions in which bacteria thrive*

Bacteria increase rapidly in a warm atmosphere, about the same
temperature as the human body. Heat can kill them and cold prevents their
multiplying. They also like moist conditions.

The foods most likely to carry infection are milk, milky puddings,
meat, gravy and cream. These are the foods in which bacteria will multiply
rapidly.

**Rules for hygienic handling of food**

1   Cook foods such as meat thoroughly to destroy bacteria.
2   If cooked food is to be stored, cool it rapidly. Do not leave it around in warm
     conditions.
3   When reheating cooked food, heat it thoroughly. Do not reheat it more than
     once.
4   Store food in a cool place, preferably a refrigerator. Do not store it for too lon
5   Always keep food covered.

**Personal hygiene of people handling food**

1   Wash your hands thoroughly with hot, soapy water before preparing food an
     always after going to the toilet. There are bacteria in the bowel which could
     otherwise be transferred to the food you eat.
2   Never lick your fingers or utensils and then put them into food. There can be
     harmful bacteria in your mouth, nose and throat.
3   Wash your hands after using a handkerchief while handling food.
4   Do not handle food if you have a heavy cold, sickness or diarrhoea.
5   Cover all cuts with a clean bandage. Replace it frequently.
6   Keep your nails clean and your hair out of food.
7   Wear a clean apron or overall.

**Cleanliness in the kitchen**

1   Keep all utensils, equipment and work surfaces clean.
2   Wash up with really hot soapy water.

3 Keep cloths used in the kitchen clean. Boil dishcloths frequently. It is much more hygienic to rinse crockery in hot water after washing up than to wipe it with a tea towel which is not absolutely clean.
4 Wrap all scraps of food and place them in a covered bin.
5 Sweep up any spilt crumbs or food. Wash the floor at least once a week.

**Cleanliness in shops**

1 Only shop in clean shops. Do not shop where assistants have low standards of hygiene, such as licking their fingers before opening paper bags, or smoking while handling food.
2 Do not shop where pets are allowed or where flies settle on food.
3 Make sure food is covered with a clean wrapping.

---

Questions

1 **What symptoms can food poisoning cause?**
2 **What are bacteria?**
3 **Describe the kind of conditions and foods in which bacteria are most likely to increase rapidly in numbers.**
4 **Why is it important to cook meat thoroughly?**
5 **What rules should you follow when reheating cooked food?**
6 **Write out five rules of personal hygiene for cooks, in order of their importance.**
7 **What are the rules to follow to ensure cleanliness in the kitchen?**
8 **Describe the unhygienic habits which assistants in food shops should avoid.**

# Further work on chapter 9

1  (a) What is meant by the term 'a well-balanced diet'?
   (b) What is the function in the body of each of the following food nutrients: protein, vitamin C, iron?
   Name one food rich in each of these nutrients.
   (c) Would you consider the following menu for a family's main meal to be well balanced?
   Fried fish in batter
   Chipped potatoes
   Creamed carrots
   Fresh fruit salad with custard.
   Give your reasons.
   (d) Give the amount of the main items in this menu, and their approximate cost, if you were purchasing for a family of four. (ALSEB)

2  (a) What is meant by a 'balanced meal'?
   (b) Give a menu for (i) a quickly prepared family supper; (ii) a slimmer's lunch.
   For each dish you choose, state the main food value. (O)

3  Correct feeding of the family is important.
   (a) Make a list of six rules to be followed when planning meals for the family.
   (b) What are the forms of malnutrition most likely to be found in the children of this country?
   (c) List the ways in which the conditions you mention can be improved.
   (d) How should you encourage children to eat foods which are good for them? (SEREB)

4  Plan meals for one day for a friend who wishes to lose weight. Make sure that you include plenty of the necessary foods, and cut down on those foods which are best avoided.

5  Why are the following important in the diet of a young child? Apples, eggs, fish, green vegetables, cereals, milk.

6  Meat is an expensive food and an excellent source of protein which is essential in the diet.
   (a) Why is it important for young children to receive an adequate supply of protein?
   (b) You cannot afford to buy any more meat this week. Suggest two evening meals which provide protein from sources other than meat.
   (c) What do you understand by the term vegetarian? What particular points have to be borne in mind when planning and serving meals for a vegetarian guest? State three suppers which you could serve to your guest.

7   You are spending the July holiday with your husband and
    two-year-old son in a caravan at the seaside. You have two boiling
    rings and a grill for cooking.
    (a) Plan the main meals for a typical day – breakfast, dinner, tea.
    (b) List the food you would take to avoid unnecessary shopping.
    (c) Name five precautions to be taken before leaving your house
    unoccupied during the holiday. (ALSEB)

8   Many different kinds of midday meal are available to a person out at
    work. The following are three examples:
    (a) Fish, chips, apple pie, tea.
    (b) Egg and cheese salad, roll and butter, orange juice.
    (c) Steak and kidney pie, yoghourt and apple.
    (i) Why would a secretary probably choose B?
    (ii) Suggest a suitable evening meal the housewife could prepare if her
    family all had meal A at midday.
    (iii) Suggest a balanced midday meal for a mother who is staying at
    home, and give reasons for your choice.
    (iv) How can the family co-operate in providing economic meals in this
    time of increasing inflation?

9   (a) The family mealtime should be a happy time. Suggest three ways
    in which you might achieve this.
    (b) List eight interesting sandwich fillings or small savouries which
    you might use when entertaining some of your friends.
    (c) Name six safety precautions to take before having a party for
    six-year-olds. List the food you would provide. Suggest four games
    you would organize. (ALSEB)

10  Convenience foods are plentiful.
    (a) What do you understand by the term 'convenience foods'?
    (b) Name two different types of convenience foods which are available
    and give one example of each.
    (c) Write two sentences about convenience foods under each of the
    following headings: (i) cost; (ii) saving of time and energy; (iii) the
    ability of the housewife; (iv) imaginative use of the products.
    (d) Which foods are date-stamped and why? (SEREB)

11  Many teenagers are overweight. What are the main causes and how
    should a diet be planned to obtain a steady weight reduction? (O)

12  Feeding the family to keep them healthy is the aim of all housewives.
    (a) State the nutrients required for a healthy skin and give two
    examples of foods for each nutrient.
    (b) Name three foods to avoid eating in excess if you want a good
    skin.
    (c) What is the importance of fibre (roughage) in the diet?
    (d) Why is it important to use the stock from the cooking of meat and
    vegetables?
    (e) List, with reasons, the best methods of cooking for retaining
    nutrients. (EAEB)

13 (a) List four ways in which strict vegetarians can obtain proteins.
(b) Plan a day's meals for a lacto-vegetarian family.
(c) How can the housewife overcome the problem of excess carbohydrate in this family's diet?
(d) What precautions should you take to avoid the destruction of Vitamin C? (EAEB)

14 A housewife needs to maintain a high standard of hygiene. Discuss this under the following headings:
(a) Rules of hygiene to be observed during the preparation of food.
(b) Considerations of hygiene when selecting shops for food purchases.
(c) Encouraging children to develop good habits of hygiene.
(d) The contribution to good hygiene in the home and community by the local authority. (MREB)

15 (a) List six general points which must be considered when planning meals.
(b) List eight additional points which could be of particular assistance with meal planning at a time when food prices are rising. (SCE)

16 (a) The rising cost of living makes careful budgeting necessary for the housewife. Suggest ways in which a housewife could economize in her food bill.
(b) Comment on the following menus in relation to the saving of fuel.

| Menu A | Menu B |
|---|---|
| Grilled steak and tomato | Lamb casserole with carrots |
| Boiled potatoes | Baked potatoes |
| Apple sponge and custard | Apple tart and cream |

(c) Suggest additional ways of cutting down the fuel bill when cooking.
(d) What special adjustments should be made to family meals when the family includes a toddler? Give reasons for your answers. (SCE)

Books for further reading

*Manual of Nutrition* **H.M.S.O.**
*Success in Nutrition* **Magnus Pyke** John Murray
*Food Science* **Birch, Cameron and Spencer** Pergamon
*O-level Cookery* **Abbey and Macdonald** Methuen Educational
*Eat your way to Health* **Jill Leslie and David Lewis** Aidfairs Ltd.

Chapter 10
# Work and leisure

# Choosing a career

Your last year at school is a good time to start finding out about future careers and employment.

**Careers teacher**

Many schools have a teacher especially concerned with careers. He or she will be able to give you information and advice about the kind of job you feel would suit your interests and ability. He will be able to tell you what subjects at school will be most useful to you for a certain job, what particular qualifications you will need from school and whether a job has good prospects of promotion. The careers teacher is always available to give information and advice on any problems or questions you may have about work or training. Often, he or she will arrange for people from different industries or occupations to give talks at school, to tell you what is involved in their own kind of work, so that you can make a better choice.

## Careers Officer

Every Local Education Authority has a Careers Officer concerned with giving guidance to school-leavers. He or she will often visit the school in the last few months before you leave to give a general talk to all the pupils. He may have an individual interview later with each school leaver where he will discuss with you and your parents the kind of work that you would like and may make suggestions about the jobs and training that are available.

The Careers Officer will know about the particular employment situation in your area and will help you apply for a particular job. Usually you make contact with the Careers Officer through school, but you can also contact him directly at the local Careers Office or Job Centre, the address of which will be in the telephone book. Not only will he help you find your first job, but he will help with any work or career problem throughout the first few years after leaving school or college.

## Training

The Careers Office can advise you about applying for apprenticeships and other training schemes for different trades or occupations.

## Further Education

Many courses are available at colleges to those over sixteen years old. They usually involve training or education for a particular kind of work, for example secretarial courses, pre-nursing courses, child-care, hairdressing, catering, and building trade or engineering courses. Students can attend these colleges for a year or two or they can take a part-time day or evening course. A part-time course might involve working for four days a week and attending college one day a week as part of an apprenticeship scheme.

Usually, the more training you have to develop your skills and gain qualifications, the more likely it is that you will eventually find a career which will be interesting and enjoyable and where prospects of promotion are good.

---

Questions

1  **When should you start thinking about a career?**
2  **List some of the ways in which the careers teacher at school could help you.**
3  **Why do Careers Officers visit schools in the few months before you leave school?**
4  **How could you get in contact with the Careers Officer in your area?**
5  **How can a Careers Officer help you?**
6  **What kind of educational courses do Further Education colleges offer to students?**
7  **Why should you consider taking a Further Education course?**

# Interviews

When you first apply for a job it will usually be by letter in response to an advertisement in the paper, or through the Careers Officer.

The employer will probably receive several letters, and using them as a guide he will select some of the applicants to come for an interview. You want your letter to be selected as one of the best written so that you will have an interview, so take care to write a good letter in your best handwriting.

Use plain, good quality writing paper without lines and write in your own handwriting. A fine felt-tipped pen, or a fountain pen, usually produces better writing than a ball-point pen.

A sample letter is shown below. The general pattern would be the same if you were applying for a place on a college course.

> 25, Long Avenue,
> Newton,
> FE2 5XJ
> June 27th, 1980
>
> Dear Sir,
>
> I would like to apply for the position of junior typist with your company, as advertised in 'The Daily News' of June 26th.
>
> I am 16 years old, leaving St. Robert's School, Newton, in July this year. I expect to have six C.S.E. passes, including typing, commerce and English.
>
> I should be pleased to supply any further information you require, or to attend for interview at any time.
>
> Yours faithfully,
> J. Brown (Miss)
>
> The Manager,
> Sun Electricals Ltd.,
> Newton

Before you are offered a job or place in college, you will nearly always have to attend an interview. The impression you make can be very important in deciding whether or not you are offered the place.

## Appearance

Take particular care with your appearance. You want to give your prospective employer a good impression and to look as though you will take your work seriously. You should try to look well groomed, neat and tidy, rather than way-out and extremely fashionable. Make sure that your shoes are well polished and your clothes well brushed and clean. Do not wear a lot of perfume, make-up or jewellery and keep your hair in a neat, tidy style.

Try to appear calm and confident even though you may be feeling nervous. If you are introduced to someone, smile and say 'Hello' or 'How do you do?' Be ready to shake hands if required.

A few days before the interview think about the questions you may be asked, and have some ideas ready. You may be asked why you want the job, or whether you would be prepared to study at afternoon or night classes to improve your skill at the job.

The interview is the time for you to ask any questions you have, perhaps about the work involved, salary, prospects of promotion, training schemes, hours or holidays. These will show that you are interested in the job. Speak clearly and be polite and well-mannered, and let the employer see that you will be an asset to his or her staff!

## Questions

1 **Why is it important to write your letter of application carefully?**
2 **What kind of paper and pen will give a good impression to a possible employer?**
3 **Write a letter similar to the one shown above, applying for a job you would like.**
4 **Write a letter to a college, enquiring about night classes in a subject which interests you. You should address your letter to 'The Principal'.**
5 **You have been asked to go for an interview for a job in a department store or office. Describe how you would dress. List some of the clothes you would not wear on this occasion.**
6 **Write down three of the questions which (a) you might be asked at the interview, and (b) you would ask about the job.**

# The community and you

A community is a group of people living in the same area. It includes everyone in that area, families, single people, old people, teenagers, children and babies.

Most of the people in any community can do something to contribute to the feeling of community spirit and friendliness in the neighbourhood which helps to make people feel settled and 'at home', and part of the place they live in.

There are community centres in many areas where people can take part in all kinds of different activities. They provide a place and an opportunity for people of all ages to meet socially and to enjoy their leisure time in various ways.

The recreation and leisure activities in community centres could include playgroups, Youth Clubs, Bingo sessions, table tennis, classes in different subjects such as painting, local history, home maintenance, soft furnishings, and also dances, discos, whist drives and social clubs for old people.

### Clubs and societies

Clubs and societies exist for people with all kinds of interests, from cycling to dressmaking, from judo to musical appreciation, from chess to growing leeks. Most libraries keep a list of the societies and organizations in their locality. See what appeals to you and go along. There are always plenty of interesting things going on if you look for them.

### Museums and art galleries

Museums and art galleries often have societies catering for anyone interested in their particular subject, perhaps natural history or local history. Sometimes they are glad of offers of voluntary help for some of their routine work, or they may provide the opportunity for a working holiday such as an archaeological 'dig' or a conservation project.

**The Youth Hostels Association**
Address: Trevelyan House, St Albans, Hertfordshire

The YHA exists to provide people of all ages, though mainly young people, with the opportunity of really cheap holidays and weekends. They have hostels in most parts of the country where members can stay overnight for a very low charge. Meals are provided in some hostels, or you can cook your own food in the members' kitchens, which is even cheaper.

**Further Education**

There are Further Education centres in all areas. They run classes in a wide variety of subjects for anyone over school-leaving age. Courses may be full or part-time, in the day-time or evenings.

You can take courses purely for enjoyment or you can take a course leading to a certificate which could make you better qualified for a particular job.

Recreational and leisure classes are usually held in the afternoons and evenings so that both people who are out at work and housewives can take part. They could include such subjects as pottery, photography, car maintenance, keep-fit, flower arranging, dress-making, swimming or cake-icing. The choice is usually wide. Some centres will consider suggestions for a course in any subject, if enough public interest is shown.

Full-time and part-time courses can also be followed which lead to qualifications at all levels, including G.C.E. Ordinary and Advanced levels, R.S.A. commercial and secretarial courses, catering courses and courses up to degree level. Again, the range of subjects offered is usually wide and varied.

It is really worthwhile looking at the courses at Further Education centres in your area to see what they can offer you, whether it is the pleasure of a new interest or a course which could lead to a better paid and more interesting job.

Hull College of Higher and Further Education

Questions

1  **What kind of activities are normally held in a community centre?**
2  **Who can join in these activities?**
3  **Where would you find a list of the clubs and societies in your area?**
4  **What kind of courses do Further Education centres offer?**

# Voluntary organizations

Voluntary organizations exist to bring together those people needing help of some kind with people who have time and are willing to help. Voluntary workers are not paid, but they have the satisfaction of knowing that they are helping people in their community.

*The Women's Royal Voluntary Society* is one of these organizations. They provide a wide variety of services including clubs for old people, mother-and-baby groups and play-centres, Meals-on-Wheels, visiting people who cannot leave their homes through disability, visiting people in prison or in hospitals, providing transport for the elderly or disabled, help in hospitals such as running a visitors' canteen or shop, and taking library and telephone trolleys around the wards to patients.

*The British Red Cross Society* also provides many services, mainly using voluntary workers. They train nurses to assist in hospitals, they run hospital canteens for out-patients, they visit hospital patients. They provide First Aid care for many occasions. They organize clubs, clinics and holidays for the sick, the elderly or the handicapped.

Other groups include the St. John Ambulance Association and Brigade, the National Society for Mentally Handicapped Children, local hospitals' League of Friends, and groups attached to local churches, youth clubs and some schools.

There is always a need for helpers who can give free part-time help of any kind. If you feel you could offer your help but do not know whom to contact, get in touch with your local Citizens' Advice Bureau. Their address is in the telephone book. They will put you in touch with a group which will welcome your help.

## National Council for One-Parent Families
Address: 255 Kentish Town Road, London N.W.5.

The Council is concerned with helping any single parents, either fathers or mothers, and their children. The parents may be unmarried, separated, divorced or widowed. The Council can usually offer a helpful and friendly service, giving advice about housing, jobs, nursery care, adoption, homes for mothers and babies, and legal advice. They also look at the law relating to single parents and their children to see where change or reform is needed.

## Marriage Guidance Councils

The address can be found in the local telephone directory or from the Citizens' Advice Bureau. Marriage Guidance Councils exist to help couples having problems of any kind in their marriage. Anyone who wishes to can discuss problems with a trained counsellor, knowing that anything they say will be kept in complete confidence.

The Council also publishes leaflets and books on all different aspects of marriage. There are many branches throughout the country.

### The Samaritans

The address and phone number can be found in the telephone directory. Anyone who feels distressed or unhappy and who wants someone to talk to can ring the Samaritans. They have a 24-hour service to answer all telephone calls and are always willing to listen sympathetically and let you talk about your worries. They treat all calls in confidence; you do not need to give your name unless you want to. You can arrange to visit them if you wish, so that you can talk in person to one of their counsellors. The Samaritans rely on voluntary help to keep their service going.

There is someone to talk to
**the samaritans**

---

Questions

1 **What are voluntary organizations?**
2 **Name some of the more important services of the W.R.V.S.**
3 **If you wanted to do some voluntary work, how would you get in touch with people needing your help?**
4 **Describe in your own words the work done by:**
a **The National Council for One-Parent Families**
b **The Marriage Guidance Council**
c **The Samaritans.**

# Further work on chapter 10

1  (a) How can people, including married women with children, use some leisure time to continue their education or learn some new skills?
   (b) Name two voluntary organizations. Give examples of the work they do. (ALSEB)

2  Growing old brings many problems and some hardship. List four ways in which you could help local pensioners.

3  Find out about one of the voluntary organizations in your area. Try to arrange a visit to them and describe the work they do.

4  What kind of voluntary help is available for:
   (a) a young couple experiencing marriage problems
   (b) single parents?

5  You will soon be looking for a job in readiness for when you leave school. How will you set about finding more details of the type of work in which you are interested?

   When you are called for an interview what special attention will you pay to your clothes and appearance? (O)

6  (a) How can you make the best impression at your first interview by a prospective employer?
   (b) Describe three leisure-time activities available to you in your area.
   (c) Suggest clothing to take on a weekend stay with a friend.
   (d) Write a letter to your friend's parents thanking them for the enjoyable weekend. (EAEB)

7  Write five points on each of the following:
   (a) The importance of choosing one's friends carefully.
   (b) Living with an elderly grandparent.
   (c) Maintaining a good relationship with one's parents.
   (d) How you, as a teenager, can take your share of responsibilities in the home. (EMREB)

---

**Books for further reading**

*Consumer's Guide to the British Social Services* **P. Willmot** Pelican
*Caring for the Elderly* **Gladys Francis** International Ideas
*Guide to the Social Services* Family Welfare Association

# Index